Good Will Toward Men

Women Talk Candidly About the Balance of Power Between the Sexes

Jack Kammer

St. Martin's Press · New York

11-29-01

Editor: Jared Kieling
Production Editor: Richard Klin
Copyedited by Eivind Boe
Design by Judith A. Stagnitto

Library of Congress Cataloging-in-Publication Data

Kammer, Jack.
    Good will toward men / Jack Kammer.
        p.   cm.
    ISBN 0-312-10471-5
    1. Sexism—United States.   2. Feminism—United States.
3. Men—United States—Psychology.   I. Title.
HQ1237.5.U6K36   1994
305.3'0973—dc20   93-44905
                                                          CIP

First Edition: February 1994
10 9 8 7 6 5 4 3 2 1

Books are available in quantity for promotional or premium use. Write to Director of Special Sales, St. Martin's Press, 175 Fifth Avenue, New York, NY 10010, for information on discounts and terms, or call toll-free (800) 221-7945. In New York, call (212) 674-5151 (ext. 645).

to Wild Bill & Shrimp
Nana Ardie & Pop Pop
Nana Rosie ("Dear Lord, send me a man")
my siblings, nieces and nephews
my aunts, uncles and cousins
my brothers- and sisters-in-law
—my Family

The dialogue has gone on too long in terms of women alone. Let men join women in the center of the second stage.

—Betty Friedan,
Redbook, May 1980

. . . .

[O]ne societal hallmark of self-esteem seems to be an ability to both give and demand fairness. . . . I gradually began to notice that many of the people I had been brought up to envy and see as powerful—mostly men from groups who were supposed to be the givers of approval—actually had the other half of the same problem I was experiencing. I had been raised to assume all power was outside myself, but they had been raised to place power almost nowhere but within themselves. Often they were suffering, too. Just as the fantasy of no control was the enemy of my self-esteem, the fantasy of total control was the enemy of theirs.

—Gloria Steinem,
Revolution from Within

. . . .

When a person speaks their truth, there are growing pains. As men speak their truth, there will be problems for some women. For others this will be a welcome relief, because when a person speaks their truth, the potential for intimacy becomes so much greater.

—Jean Shinoda Bolen, M.D.,
Author of *Goddesses in
Everywoman* and
Gods in Everyman

. . . .

Wars are caused not by conflict, but rather by the avoidance of conflict.

—Michael Meade

Contents

(only the briefest description of each woman and one of her topics is listed here)

Acknowledgments

This book required a lot of help. I am indebted to many people:

- the women whose ideas appear in the book
- the women who expressed good will toward men, but whose ideas I was unable, for space limitations, to include: Ellie Bragar, Deborah Cady, Carol Cassell, Susan Deitz, Dorothy Gilliam, Kay Haugaard, Linda Kelm, Careen Mayer, Marcia Singer
- Beth Trollinger, Bernardine Brooks, Kimberly Ann Porte, Barbara Dorries for tirelessly transforming tapes to transcripts
- my father for instilling the urge to do what's right
- my mother for helping a certain little boy feel he could do whatever he really wanted
- my brother Jerry, the Nieman Fellow, who demonstrated that writing was something a Kammer could do
- Gene August, Asa Baber, Jean Paul Bonhomme, Jimmy Boyd, Don Chavez, Ferrel Christensen, Gordon Clay, Jim Cook, Dick Doyle, Warren Farrell, Mel Feit, Herb Goldberg, John Gordon, Lyman Grant, Dave Gross, Richard Haddad, Fred Hayward, Ron Henry, Gene Hopp, Aaron Kipnis, David Levy, Hugh Nations, John Rossler, Jon Ryan, Jim Sniechowski, Tom Williamson, Frank Zepezauer and our necessarily anonymous social policy Deep Throat in the federal government for their insights, information and inspiration

- J.P.T. for walking with me into the woods
- Warren Farrell for giving me a map and being my guide
- Jared Kieling, my editor, and his assistant editor Ensley Eikenburg for taking me into The City and dressing me up
- Bob Frenier, Chris Harding, Dick Halloran, and the Seattle Men's Council for making my meeting with Jared possible
- Tony Falbo, Joel Vazquez and Jim English at WCVT-FM (now WTMD)
- Alice Cherbonnier of the *Baltimore Chronicle* for publishing my early columns on gender issues
- the reference librarians at Enoch Pratt Free Library (Baltimore City) and Baltimore County Public Library
- the folks at 21214 and the carriers from 21218
- Rick and Virginia Kammer of the Inn at Hamilton Field
- John Clark and George Geary of Radio Shack for technical assistance
- Kim Dockman of Travel One for travel plans
- Michael R. Harrison, who said, "First, double click here"

and mostly Karen, for being so beautiful to me

Introduction

The purpose of Good Will Toward Men is to help defuse tensions between women and men. I will be happy if readers derive insights that assist them in finding and fostering healthy romance, but I will be infinitely more fulfilled if it can help correct some of our nation's monstrous social maladies—the fragility of its families, the twisted views of manhood and womanhood our children are learning, the seething psychosexual anger and cynicism that is sapping our American optimism, joy, confidence and vigor.

America's most intractable social problems, commonly ascribed to racism and economic disadvantage, may in fact also be based on other forms of prejudice and impoverishment. It seems quite clear that many of the men who are packing our prisons, who arrived there after wreaking violence, mayhem, pain and social discord, did not end up in jail because they, as men, "have all the power." It seems instead that in a society that tells them they are nothing unless they have power—power very narrowly defined in economic and political terms—they either (1) attempted to steal, counterfeit or otherwise fake some, or (2) exploded with the frustration of having none even while being told they "have it all." Clearly, something in addition to racism and economic hardship is at work in the problems of men in the underclass. Their problems affect us all.

I believe we can trace the woeful decline in American society back to the 1960s, and in large part to the ascendancy of the notion that men, especially in family life, are disposable at best, and the embodiment of all that is harmful at worst.

For thirty years we've heard an articulation of male-female issues primarily from a female point of view. Feminism is dominating the gender issues agenda by demanding and achieving wide consideration of such questions as "who has better jobs?" "who earns more money?" "how can we make men pay more child support?" and "who is in Congress?" The recent book *Women Respond to the Men's Movement* clearly demonstrates modern feminism's reluctance to expand the inquiry to include other questions, such as "who lives happier, richer, warmer, more connected, more fulfilling lives?" "what is power, anyway?" "don't children need anything from their fathers other than money?" and "why is no one in Congress willing and able to see and address the problems facing men?" When I read *Women Respond to the Men's Movement*, the title of another neo-feminist volume—*Backlash*—came ironically to mind.

To achieve better understanding and cooperation, to promote love and respect between women and men, we must disabuse ourselves of the notion that women are the only gender with valid items for the agenda, and that men constitute the only sex that has advantages to share. An image that often pops into my head is of women and men sitting across from each other at a negotiating table. The females are pointing at the males and saying "You do this wrong, you do this wrong, and you do this wrong. And to correct it you need to give us this, give us this and give us this." Men are crossing their arms and turning away. "Okay, what's in it for us?" is the natural and healthy question that seems never to have been answered, primarily because men have never thought or felt free to ask it.

Besides, men are largely unable even to articulate what it is that they would like to have coming their way across the negotiating table. Women's domination of the public discussion of gender issues has made it nearly impossible for men—individually or collectively —to consider their needs. Men do not address the fact that they commit suicide four times more often than women, that men die seven years younger than women, that men are more likely to be alcoholic and abusive of drugs, that men often don't know their kids, that men's lives often are empty, mechanical and cold.

But men know deep in their hearts that one of the greatest shams ever concocted is the notion that by virtue of their gender they enjoy lives of power and privilege while women live lives of un-mitigated degradation and oppression.

Notice that a few paragraphs ago I said, "For thirty years we've heard an articulation of male-female issues primarily from a female point of view." I did not say "feminist point of view." The feminist perspective is not the only female outlook that holds great sway in America. Feminists and conservative women like Phyllis Schlafly may think of each other as enemies, but they both focus on wom-en's wants and needs. The conservative women's agenda, because it is supported by the status quo, is stated not as questions, challenges or demands, but as calm assertions of immutable fact. We often hear conservative women state with equanimity that "women's es-sential nature is to nurture" and "women instinctively know what is best for children and families" and "men were put on this earth to be good providers." Curiously, feminism, pursuing its unacknowl-edged backlash against men's incipient inquiry into their situation, seems to be reembracing the prerogatives of motherhood and the exclusively economic focus on fatherhood, especially where divorce forces the questions of fairness, equality and the proper roles of men and women. This alignment of conservatism and feminism has left little room for people of progressive mind on issues of gender. We must carve out new territory in which men's concerns—such as the ones discussed in this book—can be given due consideration.

Why, you might ask, must women be involved in initiating this process? If men really need a change, why don't they just make it happen? The answer lies in a paradox. It could plausibly be ar-gued—and it is, in fact, often said—that the reason only a few men are speaking up on the issues of their gender is that most men feel there is nothing to say, there are no problems. The premise of this book, however, is that the reason most men are not speaking up is *precisely because* there is so much to talk about. One of the things that most needs to be talked about is what keeps men from talking.

We would recognize the folly of mistaking a maximum security prison for a country club: "Nobody is leaving. It must be awfully nice in there." Men, I would submit, are in the most maximum security prison of all, the prison that convinces its inmates that they are right where they want to be, that they are perfectly and enviably positioned to achieve all the success they want, that as economic providers they are admired, loved and appreciated, and that if they ever begin to think otherwise, they must have a "personal" problem to be denied and buried in shame.

The oft-stated notion that women's work is undervalued has a corollary: men's work is overvalued. Society's ancient, single-minded focus on survival and efficiency viewed men's difficult and lonely struggles on the front lines of production, protection and competition as absolutely essential. Perhaps because men's traditional work is often inherently stressful and unrewarding in any spiritual or emotional sense, society must rely on customs and mores to rigorously enforce and persuasively induce men's attendance to their narrow range of duties. Words like "failure" and "loser" suggest the power of enforcement. "Money" concisely names the inducement.

On the other hand, perhaps women's traditional work of tending the homefire with the children is seen as inherently attractive and rewarding. Perhaps society is less in need of endowing it with artificial "value" to induce women to perform it, and is less insistent that women "prove" their womanhood by submitting to it. Perhaps society is less apprehensive about women experimenting with alternatives to "women's work" than it is about men exploring different ways of being "manly." Perhaps that is why women have been freer than men to talk about "choices" and have been able to achieve the widespread expansion of their gender roles we have seen in the past thirty years.

The question now is: what will women do with their ever-growing freedom? I am optimistic that women of good will, once they see the "male bastion" for what it is, will toss men the key: "Hey, snap out of it! That's no country club you're in. We'll still love you if you leave it. We'll adjust. We want our men to be alive and free." But to the extent that women harbor doubts that they really want men to unlock their lives, to the extent that men perceive that women love them for staying where they are and doing what they do, men are unlikely to be convinced that freedom and options will bring them happiness. We need assurance that we can venture forth without losing women's love and acceptance.

Another reason women must be involved in the discussion of men's gender-based social concerns is that in discussions of sexism, men are the suspect class; we have been effectively defined as the enemies of gender justice. The women in *Good Will Toward Men* are helping to provide credibility for a new male-friendly agenda, and are suggesting actions and attitudinal changes that will make a real difference in relationships between women and men. While reading this book, you might feel like a fly on the wall, eavesdropping on conversations about some of the most complex, confounding, fascinating, emotional and crucial issues facing women and men, indeed, all of American society today. If so, you might feel like a fly with opinions, experiences, attitudes and insights of your own. You might find yourself saying, "Wait, but what about . . ." and "Don't say that! Say this."

I find myself thinking the same things every time I look through the book. The interplay of gender issues between women and men generates an almost infinite network of thoughts, associations and lines of reasoning. None of these conversations would happen the same way twice.

If you adhere to feminism as "the pursuit of more rights for women," rather than "the pursuit of equal rights between the sexes," you will find this an exceedingly difficult book to stay with. I ask you please to resist saying, "Yes, but what about [a problem women face] . . ." and to devote your attention at least momentarily to the problems men endure. This book's purpose is not to be in and of itself a balanced discussion of sexism; its purpose is to redress a much larger—societal—imbalance on that terribly complex subject. Few of this book's 78,000 words are devoted to restating the very real problems of sexism against women, about which millions upon millions of words have been written. No one connected to this book denies or has forgotten the existence of sexism against women. We are attempting only to understand and demonstrate that sexism is a reciprocating engine.

The women who participated in the creation of *Good Will Toward Men* are heroes to me. I am grateful for their courage and magnanimity.

I owe it to them to make it perfectly clear that they have participated independently. Only one of the women knew the content of the conversations I had with any of the others, and she knew of only three. Any reader who is of a mind to criticize certain portions of this book should let his or her criticism be focused. The only idea we know with certainty that these women hold in common is a desire to find new approaches to old problems between women and men.

Each woman in the book had the right to approve the final version of her chapter. But rather than edit these dialogues extensively—a process that could go on forever—we cleared up the syntax a little, rearranged a few sections, and let them go, even if some of the things we said or the ways we said them surprised even us. The dialogues are intended as food for thought, as starting points rather than as academically rigorous expositions or the final word on any topic.

About me, you should understand that I have long had an abiding interest in what are described in shorthand as "men's issues." My first conscious effort in the field was *In a Man's Shoes*, a radio talk show I started on the station at Towson State University near Baltimore, in 1983. In retrospect, I know that I've been concerned about sexism against males for a long, long time. I always knew, for instance, that there was something not quite flattering in the "compliment" I often heard in my youth: "You're really good with babies—for a boy."

Since developing a conscious awareness of the effects of sexism on men, I had a sixteen-month stint as the executive director of the National Congress for Men (now the National Congress for Men and Children), an organization dedicated to "preserving the promise of fatherhood" after divorce. Though never married and not a father, I understood intuitively that parenting was a central issue for men, in much the same way that earning money was crucial to women. As executive director of the National Congress for Men, I could feel the pain of childless fathers—and dealt firsthand with the anger their pain can generate.

I also developed a part-time career as a free-lance writer "specializing in gender-based social problems." And, in 1991, a few friends and I established the Greater Baltimore Commission for Men, a nongovernmental body whose purpose was "to bring awareness of male gender issues to social policy-making, and to raise public awareness of the existence and consequences of antimale bias and stereotyping of men and boys." The support we had hoped to elicit for GBCM never materialized, and we disbanded fifteen months later.

With this background, I interviewed the women in this book not as a disinterested observer, but as a person whose feeling for the social significance of men's issues is deep.

I hope this book will help convince men that it is okay to talk to women across the sometimes fiery gulf between the sexes, that women of good will can listen open-mindedly, and that we can reverse the vicious cycle of injury, accusation and noncommunication women and men are in today.

I hope this book will encourage women of good will to become more vocal in their conversations with other women who are trapped in the old mentality of concentrating only on their half of the gender dynamic.

I hope this book will provide impetus to American men to expand the process of talking among themselves about the predicament of their gender. Strengthening the culture, pride, and ethos of healthy masculinity is crucial to the healing of our nation.

Prologue

One day a few years ago, I was talking about gender issues with a friend of mine. "Did you ever notice," he asked, "that we have the word *misogyny* to denote anger at women, but we don't have a word—except *misandry*, which no one knows or uses—for anger at men?"

"Yes, I have," I answered. "Isn't that something?"

"It sure is," he responded. "It just proves that in this man's world, being angry at men is simply not allowed."

Surprised, I said, "Gosh, I came to an entirely different conclusion."

"How could you possibly come to a different conclusion?" he asked. "It's obvious."

"Well," I began, "what's the word for crossing the street against a light or in the middle of a block?"

"That's *jaywalking*," he answered.

"And what's the word for crossing the street at an intersection with a green light?"

"There isn't any word for that. It's just called *crossing the street*."

"And so maybe," I suggested, "the reason we have a word to spotlight anger at women is because we want to punish and discourage it, and the reason we don't have a word for anger at men is because, like crossing the street with a green light, it has complete social sanction."

My friend had no response—other than to insist that surely I must be wrong.

Cathy Young

CATHY YOUNG is a free-lance writer specializing in women's issues. Her work has appeared in the *Washington Post*, the *Wall Street Journal, Reason* and *The New Republic*.

She is the author of *Growing Up in Moscow*, a memoir of her life before she emigrated from the Soviet Union to the United States at the age of sixteen. In 1992 she became one of the cofounders of the Women's Freedom Network, an organization of "dissident feminists." Cathy was born in 1963.

Jack: *You consider yourself a feminist?*

Cathy: Yes, I do.

Are there feminists who might quarrel with you?

I think there are feminists and nonfeminists who would quarrel with me. I was talking to a man about women's issues and when I said I was a feminist, he said, "No, you're not. You're not biased against men. You're not a male-basher."

So, some people would not consider me a feminist because they associate feminism with something negative. On the other hand, some feminists would not consider me a feminist because they, too, associate feminism with male-bashing—only they think male-

A simple format is used to present the dialogues: my words are shown in italic type, and those of the women are shown in roman type.

bashing is good. They would say that because I don't automatically assume that women are always oppressed by men and are always victims of men, and don't always take the woman's side in any conflict between women and men, I am therefore not a feminist. I believe very strongly that people are people regardless of gender. I don't think what one is or what one does in life is primarily determined by whether you're male or female, although I do think there are some tendencies which may be biological in men and women. I think there is a great deal of overlap in these tendencies and that we are individuals first. I believe that makes me a feminist.

On the subject of feminism, what would you say to American men?

I would say that the male-bashers do not speak for all women, though they like to pretend they do, that the vast majority of women are interested in loving partnership with men. I think a lot of women today unfortunately are being seduced by the propaganda of victimhood.

One very obvious example is the crusade against sexual harassment. It started out with good intentions, as an effort to point out that if a boss pressures a woman for sexual favors, she may feel that she is not really free to refuse. But now truly trivial experiences that some women find annoying, even if most women don't, are being redefined as sexual harassment. The current radical feminist perspective on what constitutes sexual harassment is the perspective of the most vulnerable woman, which translates easily into the most hypersensitive woman.

In all fairness, one could cite cases in which valid complaints are not taken seriously, such as a recent case involving the Bureau of Alcohol, Tobacco and Firearms, in which several women apparently were quite egregiously harassed. But that's one of the dangers in the tendency to overblow trivial charges—it desensitizes people to the serious stuff. So on the one hand this is dangerous to men because it can make a paranoid woman the arbiter of a man's fate. On the other hand, it is dangerous to women because it can lead to the dismissal of serious abuse charges.

What is all this doing to efforts to establish better relationships between women and men?

A male friend of mine who teaches at a college in New York told me that he has decided that he is never going to close the door if he has a female student in his office, because of his fear of being accused of harassment. Certainly that's not very good for the woman, because instead of giving his attention to her education, his mind is going to be on protecting himself from accusations of harassment.

Also, I've heard women express concerns that they may not be invited to business conferences that include overnight trips, because the men are afraid she'll allege they made a pass at her in the hotel. Recently a male friend who works at a magazine told me very casually that he had stayed at the office with his boss working very late, until nine or ten o'clock. And then he paused and said, "I bet if I were a woman, the boss would have been afraid to do that, because he would have been worried about accusations of harassment." If a woman editor doesn't get late-night assignments, that means she's not as valuable a worker and she doesn't get promoted.

> Old-fashioned notions of propriety also work against professional women on [Capitol] Hill. Several complained that many lawmakers do not travel on business with female staff, particularly if the woman is attractive. . . .
> Others said that many lawmakers are reluctant to take female employees to working dinners or to other after-hours events. "A lot of members, especially now, given the recent scandals, are aware of 'appearances,' " [a legislative aide] said.
>
> RICHARD MORIN
> *Washington Post*
> February 21, 1993
> in a page one article alleging sexual harassment
> in Congress

You mentioned that if the professor has possible accusations of sexual harassment on his mind, it's not good for the woman student.

Obviously, it's also not good for the professor.

Could you explain that? How do you think it might damage the professor?

It just detracts from his working environment. I'll tell you a story which I witnessed myself when I was still in college in '87. I was taking a course on human sexuality and we had a young woman in the class who had appointed herself to be the feminist watchdog. She was constantly pouncing on the professor for the most idiotic things. For instance, I remember that when he was talking about something that clearly applied only to men, to some male sexual characteristics, he used the word "people." So this young woman jumps up and says "Ah hah! So you're implying that women are not people, only men are people!" Another time we were discussing sex crimes, rape in particular. Our professor said that experts believe there are several types of rapists who are motivated by different things. Some are motivated by anger toward women and the desire to humiliate and dominate them. Others are primarily motivated just by violent impulses, and also commit a lot of violence against men. Some simply are either unable or unwilling to control their sexual urges. This young woman raises her hand and says in a very, very belligerent manner, "You're glamorizing rape. You are trying to make rape sexy." She insisted that all rapists are motivated by hatred and the desire to humiliate and dominate women, and to say anything else is totally unacceptable. Later she bragged about filing a complaint against him and getting him into trouble. He had to write a lot of letters justifying his conduct and explaining why he believed it was not sexist.

As long as the radicals can get moderate women to believe that they are really fighting for women's rights, they have a winning issue. I think we need to inform both women and men about what some of the ideologues are like. For instance, how many people know that Catharine MacKinnon, who has emerged as one of the leading spokeswomen about rape and sexual harassment, has pretty much said explicitly that heterosexual sex is rape? I'm sure that if people knew she held these views, they really wouldn't be listening to what she has to say on these issues.

Yet Peter Jennings had her as one of the panelists on ABC's special on Men, Sex and Rape in May of 1992, and Tom Brokaw had her as one of NBC's lead commentators on the Thomas-Hill hearings.

That's right. And that brings me to another element of what helps radical feminists take over the field. I think a big part of it is guilt-ridden men who walk around all day apologizing for being male.

What radical-feminist allegation do you think might be most effective at inducing feelings of guilt in men?

I think there's a generalized charge of men having power over women and abusing it. Another very similar but really more far-reaching and, in my opinion, more ominous thing is the proliferation of so-called rape-prevention workshops in which male college freshmen are sometimes essentially badgered into conceding that they may have raped some of their seemingly willing sexual partners if they didn't ask for and obtain an explicit "yes."

Why is the question of the explicit "yes" not asked of all the women who have had sex?

You make a very good point. Some campus date-rape guidelines say that there has to be consent to the specific act of penetration.

The word penetration is blatantly one-sided. The only person who can penetrate is the male. Why is it that we don't talk about envelopment?

> The one-sided presentation of female forced sex incidence rates may have fostered a negative and unrealistic public perception of college students—that men are aggressive and exploitative and that women are passive and victimized. These findings suggest that reality is much more complicated: Both men and women engage in a continuum of sexually exploitative behaviors ranging from verbal pressure to use of physical restraint and force.
>
> CINDY STRUCKMAN-JOHNSON, Ph.D.
> "Forced Sex on Dates: It Happens to Men, Too"
> *The Journal of Sex Research,* Vol. 24, p. 241,
> 1988

Good point. I recently read an article in a scholarly journal which specifically considered the question of definitions of rape. Some studies define rape as any sexual acts involving drugs or alcohol—if the woman was drunk or stoned. And again, if a woman has sex with a man who is drunk, no one is asking if she raped him.

One of the major points you write about is that feminism originally talked about the need for women to get more assertive.

Sure.

Now we have a brand of feminism urging upon women the assumption of victimhood.

Absolutely. It's very gratifying to some people to turn every trivial annoyance into a cosmic drama of oppression and struggle for liberation in which they are the perfectly good, perfectly innocent, oppressed victims and the people annoying them are absolutely evil. It also exonerates them of responsibility for their actions. If a woman has had sex with a man and feels bad about it later and thinks, "Oh, I really shouldn't have had sex with that jerk," she can persuade herself that it really wasn't voluntary. He forced her and therefore she doesn't have to confront what it was about her behavior that got her into that situation. And I'm not saying, by the way, that provocative behavior on the part of the woman justifies rape. But I do think she has a responsibility to clearly make the point that she doesn't want to have sex.

I'm looking for a theme here, a key as to what is motivating this brand of feminism.

A desire for power, I think.

Why would feminism want women to be able to do whatever they want? Is it because they perceive men as being able to do whatever they want?

That's a good question. That could be the case. What is it that motivates people to seek power? I think there is such a thing as power lust. And for a certain type of personality there is great satisfaction in imposing your will on other people. I think also that some people are sincerely misguided. Some people perceive women as being victimized by men at every step in their lives. I think they are motivated by the desire to help women, but also I think some of the ideologues are seeking power not so much for women in general as for themselves and for their clique.

The new girls' network?

I guess you could call it that. Yeah, that's very much the case, especially with the women's studies phenomenon in which women are trying to dictate the curriculum and write campus codes that would turn ninety percent of the men into rapists. In my view there's good empowerment and there's bad empowerment. Good empowerment is essentially giving people power over their own lives. Bad empowerment is giving them power over other people's lives. I think that the radical feminists are interested very much in the second kind of empowerment.

Is that drive for power motivated by a belief that women should exercise power over men's lives because women are just better, they are more moral?

I think for some feminists that is the case. It amazes me, for instance, that we have a major female newspaper columnist, Anna Quindlen, who has repeatedly expressed her view that women are morally superior to men. She gets a Pulitzer prize. She is a very hot item. Now just imagine that you have a male columnist who had explicitly written of his belief that men are superior to women and should therefore be in command. He certainly wouldn't be writing a column for the *New York Times,* much less getting a Pulitzer.

In what ways does she say that women are superior to men?

During the 1992 election campaign she said, "If we really believe . . . that there's not a male politician in America who hasn't slept around, I've got a solution for the future. Look for a woman." Then she said, "If we really believe . . . that our political leaders don't have a clue about real life, look for a woman." And she said, "I've rarely met a woman who didn't know more about the supermarket, the bus stop and the prevailing winds than her male counterparts. Not to mention child care, human rights, abortion, the minimum wage and sexual harassment."*

What would you say is the best refutation of that line of thinking?

First of all, there is simply no evidence that women in office are more compassionate or more ethical than men. In fact, Carol Moseley Braun, who was elected to the Senate as part of this wave of new women, is reported to have some really big ethical problems. I'm not saying that she's unique in this, because certainly a lot of male congressmen have ethical problems. All I'm saying is she's certainly no better in that respect.

* *New York Times,* February 2, 1992

It's amazing how this is really a return to the Victorian view of woman, that women don't sleep around, even though a lot of surveys now suggest that female rates of adultery are almost as high as the rates for men. But Anna Quindlen tells us that women don't sleep around. And I might add that in states where women are represented in large numbers in the legislatures, they have been every bit as likely as men to be involved in corruption scandals. There was a case in Arizona recently where a large number of legislators were caught in a sting operation involving bribery and organized crime. Several of the major culprits in that incident were women.

Was Carol Gilligan's book the starting point, the seed of this new branch of sexist feminism?

Partially.

How would you describe the Gilligan book?

Carol Gilligan's book, *In A Different Voice*, argues that there are distinctly male and female ways of making moral judgments. That women make moral judgment based on caring for other people, caring for their needs, caring for intimacy and relationships. And men's moral judgments are based on abstract notions of people's rights as opposed to their needs.

Abstract seems like a loaded word.

Well, certainly, it is a loaded word. Abstract rights versus real needs? Which one do you prefer? Men make moral judgments based on autonomy, considering every person in a context that is isolated from other people.

That's just spin control, isn't it? Couldn't we put a negative spin on what Carol Gilligan says about the way women think and make moral judgments, and put a positive spin on what she says about the way men make moral judgments?

Certainly: men have principles and women are so eager to please others that it's the only thing they care about. This is something that feminists used to complain about—that women were socialized to please other people rather than think of their own integrity and their own personal goals. The only problem, which is highly ironic, is that the feminine traits that Carol Gilligan puts a positive spin on were also viewed very positively by the Victorians. They were seen as feminine virtues. And it was early feminists who defined these things as flaws, not male chauvinists, as the new feminists—the followers of Carol Gilligan—are claiming.

One of her contentions is that men have a fear of intimacy. But there was really only a small gap between men and women. Most of these gender gaps tend to be in the area of seven, ten, maybe fifteen percent, tops. At the most we are talking merely about tendencies in one direction or the other.

You wrote in one of your pieces that the variations inside a gender group are often as great as the variations between the groups.

Absolutely. And this is a point the earlier feminists were trying to make, that gender roles should be more flexible because individual characteristics are distributed across gender lines. But now we seem to be going in a direction of greatly exaggerating these differences and turning them into absolutes. Another pitfall of the type of research that the people like Carol Gilligan do is that they only measure the extent to which people *see themselves* as empathetic. Women tend to consider themselves more empathetic than men. But some studies have found that how people rate themselves on empathy or other traits is often almost unrelated to how much of those traits they exhibit in real life.

Suspiciously, experiments performed by women researchers have been more likely than those conducted by men to find that female subjects are especially empathic. But what seems to matter most of all is the way empathy is measured. That was the conclusion of psychologist Nancy Eisenberg and a student of hers after they reviewed more than 100 studies in 1983. "There is a huge sex difference in self-report of empathy as measured with questionnaires . . . [but] little evidence of a sex difference in physiological response to another's emotional distress," they wrote.

ALFIE KOHN
You Know What They Say . . . : The Truth About Popular Beliefs

Is it possible that what we're seeing in the phenomenon of male-bashing is a backlash on the part of women who are trying to reverse the advances of men into their traditionally female domains—that women are threatened by men wanting to be more involved in nurturance, child rearing and intimacy, for instance?

Well, they claim that they want more flexible gender roles. I don't know about MacKinnon, but Susan Faludi and Naomi Wolf do.

But don't you point out in one of your reviews of Faludi's book that she is quite gleeful about the fact that men have virtually no say in the reproductive process?

Yes, and that's where radical-feminist hypocrisy comes in. On the one hand Faludi says it is a great injustice that women are the ones who do all the child care, but at the same time she is gleeful about the fact that men are increasingly left with no say whatsoever in the reproductive process. I don't see how she can reconcile that contradiction. Basically, it's the woman who sets the rules.

The Rules

1. The FEMALE always makes the rules.
2. Rules are subject to change at any time without prior notification.
3. No male can possibly know all the rules.
4. If the FEMALE suspects that the male knows all the rules, she must immediately change some or all of the rules.
5. The FEMALE is NEVER wrong.
6. The FEMALE can change her mind at any given time.
7. The male can never change his mind without express written consent of the FEMALE.
8. The FEMALE has every right to be angry or upset.
9. If the FEMALE is wrong, it is because of a flagrant misunderstanding which is a direct result of something the male did or said.
10. If number 9 applies to you, the male must apologize immediately for causing the misunderstanding.

11. The male must remain calm at all times unless the FE-
    MALE wants him to be angry or upset.
12. The FEMALE must under no circumstances allow the
    male to know whether or not she wants him to be angry
    or upset.

Flier on executive woman's bulletin board
March 1990

Could you, as they say at college, compare and contrast radical feminism and arch-conservatism on the notion of female superiority?

On the issue of pornography we've seen an alliance between radical feminists of the Catharine MacKinnon type and people of the Fundamentalist Christian right. The impulse on the part of radical feminists in trying to censor pornography is based at least in part on their fear of and their desire to dehumanize male sexuality. Male sexuality is seen as evil.

And the men-are-beasts rhetoric is surprisingly common among some right-wingers who endorse traditional gender roles. They will sometimes say that men have uncontrollable sexual urges that will run wild unless they are domesticated by women.

I have a quote from Newt Gingrich that we'll insert here. He illustrates your point exactly.

Okay. What did he say?

One of the things that we know historically and biologically is that males are designed to be relatively irresponsible. . . . When you read about a 16-, 17-, 18-year-old kid going to jail as a criminal boasting that he's already had eleven children by ten different women, you know you have a society which is breaking down in its core values.

Congressman Newt Gingrich
Republican from Georgia
speaking on *Morning Edition*
National Public Radio
August 28, 1992

He's talking about one man and ten women being irresponsible here.
Yet there is no mention at all of female irresponsibility. Newt, wake up!

Right. And this men-are-beasts rhetoric is also used against women to control women's sexuality. The idea is that women have to be the guardians of sexual morality because men's sexual urges are uncontrollable. Because of the abortion issue, conservatives don't want to be seen as antifemale, so it's safer to bash men, I guess.

Judith Sherven

JUDITH SHERVEN, Ph.D., is a clinical psychologist whose
specialty is working with couples and individuals, both men and
women, who find it difficult to sustain intimate relationships. She
works with her husband, James Sniechowski, in gender reconciliation—helping men understand women and women understand men.
Judith lives in Los Angeles. She was born in 1943.

Jack: *Your work with women includes asking them to make some
changes other than the ones they've been demanding. What kinds of
changes do you have in mind?*

Judith: The women's liberation era was largely a political and
external movement. It had to be. But there was very little looking
inside and saying, "How is it that I am so willing to be submissive?
Why am I so willing to blame men for my condition? What am I
doing that gets in my way of breaking the Glass Ceiling in the
corporate world? Why do I refuse promotions that are offered to me?
What's getting in my way that I can't be more successful? How
come in the presence of men, I somehow turn into this little coy,
clinging girl when just a few hours ago at work I was a very strong,
opinionated woman?"

There are a lot of internal barriers that women hold about how
they think they need to be that are far more dangerous, far more
limiting than the external issues. Granted, the two areas can't be
totally separated, but the external issues are not going to change
very readily until the internal ideas have changed.

Women have been hypnotized into thinking "it's a romantic world" and that all they have to do is be pretty, sweet, nice, and cunning, and a man will save them. He'll know exactly what she wants and needs. Too many women think they don't have to get an education, they don't need a career, they don't need financial support of their own. And in fact they're often talked out of that by their parents, mostly by their mothers, because a man will "save them."

These ideas are still at work? It's 1993!

Absolutely. They're practically as present in high school girls today as they ever were. Shockingly so. The National Organization for Women criticizes the patriarchy for not granting women equal rights, equal voice and equal stature. But NOW and the radical feminists have not yet made it politically correct to analyze how mothers raise their daughters.

What needs to be examined about the way women think of themselves and the way women have been brought up?

I start with asking women how they value themselves. Largely, women are taught that their value is in getting a man, having a man pay for her, and that she has very little personal value. And she may even have a career! Women are often split. A woman may own her own business, but when it comes to a man, she's not going to share payment for dating, she won't go out with a man who doesn't make more money than she does. I can't tell you how many women in 1993 are still saying, "I want to look up to a man. I don't want to be on an equal footing with a man. It's not romantic, it's not sexy."

I have women clients who struggle, who in principle think that it's wise to share economically in dating, for instance, because then they won't feel obligated to put out sexually, but they're so embarrassed about making that transition that they frequently can't do it. They would rather be mute, be uncomfortable, have the man go ahead and pay—but at least feel they're being ladylike. They're also afraid of making the man uncomfortable, heaven forbid.

I don't know. It certainly made men uncomfortable to see women entering executive suites and police forces, but that didn't stop women from doing it. I have to wonder whether "I would do it except it would hurt the man" is a pretext for avoiding something they don't really want to do.

It has to do with her image of herself. If she thinks, "I have to appear feminine, I have to appear ladylike and demure," she's going to have a lot of trouble saying, "Thanks for dinner, and next time I'm buying." Or, "I'd like to split the check with you." But if she has already done sufficient inner work, if she thinks, "I don't want the fantasy that I'm a princess and he's a prince; I want to start my relationships on the same footing that I want with a partner— equal," then she'll act like an equal.

I can't tell you the number of single women I've had in my practice who claimed they wanted to get married, but wouldn't date anybody unless they had an income of so much, or a portfolio worth so much. Their fantasy is "When I find the right man, he will give me the right life-style. I'll have the right kind of house, I'll live in the right kind of neighborhood, I'll have so and so number of kids, they'll go to this private school." It's a romantic fantasy that women are still living in. And I'm a recovering romantic. I speak from whence I come. I didn't get married until I was forty-four, because I had to get over this stuff.

Did you get close to getting married along the way?

I was engaged, or engaged to be engaged, a couple of times, but I could see a divorce down the road, and I had no interest in that. It took a lot of work on myself to get ready to be with just a guy, and have just a life.

I can imagine it could be pretty depressing for a romantically minded but not terribly gorgeous woman to look in the mirror and think that the best prospect she's got for her economic happiness is some man who's going to be willing to settle for her mediocre looks. Any possibility that this disappointment can manifest itself in anger or rage at men?

Sure. Absolutely. But it can happen to attractive women, too. I can speak better from my own life. I worked as a model and actress most of my teens and twenties, so I am attractive, and always had men to date. Nevertheless, because I was raised with this same "find a man to take care of you" ethic, I found myself in my twenties hating men, being a version of today's male-bashers, blindly believing that it was men's fault that I felt so powerless. And I eventually went into therapy because I wasn't getting married and I couldn't understand why. I discovered that there's a part of me that has a lot of integrity and wisdom, and that I couldn't possibly get married to a man and give all my power away. So I avoided getting married, blessedly. But I then had to do the work of finding my own power, so that I wouldn't have to hate men anymore, and I wouldn't have to believe that they have all the power.

When you were hating men, what were you thinking?

That they were assholes, that they were all monsters in one form or another. They were either passive slugs, who were worthless, or they were macho jerks, who were useless.

And they all wanted to get in your pants.

They either wanted to get in my pants, or they didn't want to get in my pants, and that was boring.

While you were hating men, and thinking contemptuous thoughts of men, were you also dating them?

Oh, yes, of course! And I was in great competition with them in raging arguments about politics or—it didn't matter what the topic was, the issue was to try to beat them, to try to show them that I actually did have power. It was all unconscious, but I spent a lot of time arguing and shouting and trying to prove that I was smart and they weren't so smart.

As you look back now, do you see anything different about them and power?

I see that what looked so powerful then was *my* lack of internal comfort, so that when I looked at them, they looked comfortable. I still know some of these men; I now know that they were struggling with their own issues. But I couldn't see that because that wasn't what I was looking for. I was looking for them to be the Rock of Gibraltar. I was expecting them to be the potential prince who might come along and rescue me. I didn't want to see any faults or flaws. It would have wrecked my fantasy about them being the prince.

There's a lot of press about male violence against women, but one of the things we don't look at is a sort of soul violence that women carry toward men when they imagine they've married a prince. As the actual man shows up, the rage that women feel over the disappointment of not getting a prince can be vicious. I'm speaking for I can't tell you how many couples I've seen in my office. The women do not feel that they're being violent or vicious or destructive when they lambaste their men for not being their fantasy ideal. They believe, in some unconscious manner, that they really are entitled to the prince, and it's okay to abuse this guy because he's not perfect.

And does the guy being abused see himself being unjustly abused or does he see himself being justly criticized for being a failure?

It depends again on the level of consciousness of the man. I've seen both, many, many times.

If a man believes himself to be a failure, can that paralyze him so that he doesn't defend his integrity?

That's what I've seen. Many men become mute, because some part of them thinks they're supposed to be the prince also, and that they should be able to make a woman happy.

I think I can convince men that this romantic ideal is a pretty rough deal for them. If all you're good for is your money, you've got to work a lifetime for it, and there's never enough. If I were a woman, what would you say to convince me that I've also got a lot of reasons to abandon this situation? What's to keep me from thinking, "Why should I change? This is great for me. All I've got to do is look good and I get this guy to go out and kill himself to make money that I get to enjoy?"

Women I've had in my office, who have no hope of having real love in their lives, would agree. "I am staying with this program completely. It works for me. I don't expect to be loved. I don't think men can love anyway. So I might as well have the money." But if I can appeal to women beyond that cynicism and injury, I can get them to see that money can never provide the kind of emotional sustenance that they're hoping to get as well.

What typically has happened along the way for a woman to get to the point where she thinks, "I don't think men can love anyway"?

Chances are she was raised by a mother who had a rotten marriage herself, who did not know how to take care of herself within her marriage, did not speak up for herself in the marriage, and so the mother has passed down to the daughter a cynicism and bitterness about men, and very often has passed down the message that "it's just as easy to love a rich man."

Let's imagine that you have a new female client. Make her Everywoman. She comes to you with a typical complaint about her life, and she has the typical complaints about men. What would that typical presentation be?

She's been going with a man for six months, she's been married twice before, she has an interest in eventually marrying again, but she's concerned that he doesn't want to be committed. "You know how men are, they don't ever want to commit."

One second. I want to say to this woman, "You're divorced twice! What are you saying about commitment?" Does she recognize the anomaly here?

Chances are, if she's Everywoman, she'll say, "But you don't understand. I was devoted, I was a wonderful wife, I was there, I made dinner, you can see I'm an attractive woman, I gave him everything that I could. But the first one was a drunk, and the second one ran off with a floozy. I don't seem to be able to find a decent man. They don't want to be committed."

So I would begin with, "Let's look at how you seem to give yourself away. What you've just told me is that you have done everything to keep the men, but you didn't keep them. They left you. They weren't interested."

So when she says, "He wasn't there for me," does the question become, "Well, where was 'there' and where were you?"

Exactly. How would he know that you needed anything? How would he ever have the information that you were unhappy with how things were going? "Well, I don't want to be a nag." Or, "I don't want him to feel henpecked." Or, "My mother said that men don't like women who complain all the time."

What's the difference between henpecking and stating your needs?

I think the best way to distinguish it is that henpecking occurs when a woman asks but believes that she's still not going to get what she wants.

He's guilty before she gives him a chance.

Exactly. And she doesn't ask for it in a forthright, direct, bold, serious manner. She asks for it from a victimized, whiny, nyeh-nyeh-nyeh tone of voice that does not inspire him to do it.

There were women's consciousness groups, particularly about how not to be oppressed in marriage, but again, women still haven't done the internal work. I've seen it in my own marriage, after all the work I've done on myself, after spending my life on these issues. Particularly when I was first married, I would find myself talking baby talk to ask for something. And Jim hated it. He'd say, "Why are you talking baby talk? Tell me straight; what is it you want?" Or I'd find myself sort of couching my question around a corner, and subtly getting it in there, "Well, would you maybe, could you possibly . . . ?" and he'd say "What? That's so annoying! What do you want? Just tell me!" I feel like I speak for a lot of women on this. And it took some real consciousness and some real awareness to just ask a man as I would ask another woman.

I can understand the factor of a woman feeling powerless so that she has to shuck and jive to get the man to do what she wants him to do. But on the other hand, I can see that part of what justifies or what motivates her to be indirect is that she doesn't want to honor, respect and solicit his input to the situation. She knows what's right, and any way she can get it done is justifiable.

It's curious, isn't it, that as powerless as women have been trained to be, in the area of domestic relations there's also a kind of entitlement and righteousness that women have passed down. If the woman has the unilateral attitude that it's "my way or the highway," and we start seeing men take the highway, we have to take a look and say, "This cannot be all men's fault." And for a lot of these men there may be wisdom in taking the highway.

In the woman's mind, what justifies her righteousness?

The first thing that comes to mind is that a lot of women think that men are boys, that men are really not grown up, they are not responsible, they're not organized, that they expect to be taken care of. We women, on the other hand, know how to take care of things. We're on the ball, we've got things taken care of; you're off playing softball with the boys.

And, of course, if you're female, you know all about intimacy; you're really skilled with intimacy. There's a lot of prejudice and mythology that has to be taken apart here, because I don't see that women are any more emotionally available than men. Truly. They may be able to cry more easily, just like men can get angry and rage more easily. But when it comes down to actually telling their truth, their emotional truth, to a man they care about, I don't see that women can do it any better than men can do it with women. And I'm saying that after seventeen years of doing counseling and psychotherapy and who-knows-how-many seminars and conferences.

Why are men not saying, "Knock it off!" when women assume undue control of the relationship?

I think we have to look at what's considered manly. Within the confines of masculinity as it's been structured, up until recently, it has not been manly to object to how a woman treats a man. Men are supposed to be able to tolerate anything; they are tough, they can take anything.

Especially from this insignificant little creature called a woman. This little ball of fluff.

Precisely. So to object would require him to say, "I don't like how this is. I'm not so tough, and not so strong; I'm getting hurt."

Or "I am strong. I am tough. But guess what? You're strong, and you're tough, too."

That would be wonderful. That's what it needs to be. The word that works for me, for both genders, is for us to be able to be fierce together, so that I don't have to worry that if I hurt your feelings by objecting to something, you're going to fall over dead or fly into a rage. And I don't want you to worry when you get fierce and object to something about me, that I'm going to collapse in a puddle of tears, or faint, or go flying out the door to mother's house. Both genders need to have enough internal substance that we can really take each other on when we need to.

Men have trouble putting their finger on women's strength and power. It's like Miss Piggy the Muppet saying "Moi?" There's no vocabulary for talking about women's power. It's easy to deny. We need a vocabulary for tagging, discussing and calling women's power into account.

> The notion of giving something a *name* is the vastest generative idea that was ever conceived.
>
> SUZANNE K. LANGER
> as quoted by Gloria Steinem
> in *Revolution from Within*

What comes to mind are two points. One is that we need some language about the power of the powerless, or the power of victimization. We don't have acceptable language for that because in today's political climate you can't blame the victim. Number two, we need to be able to discuss the kind of power that women have in the example we were using earlier, when they assume they're not going to get what they are asking for, so they make the man bad or wrong at the outset. That's power, the power of shame, perhaps. The other matter here is how to help women become conscious that they're doing it. It would be best if the man could spot a particular behavior and point it out immediately. "Look, right at this minute, this is power. You just announced what was appropriate to wear to church."

He's going to have to stop pretending that these "little things" that really bother him don't really bother him.

Precisely.

So if he feels bothered, he should trust his feelings, and say, "Excuse me, I don't know exactly what's going on here, but we have something to talk about."

Right. And remind the woman, "You've been asking me to speak my feelings. I want you to take me seriously. I am now telling you a feeling."

I wonder if part of the reason that men don't communicate emotional things to women is because women don't really want to be faced with the ugly emotional realities of men's lives.

I think that's really well put. Again, it's this issue of romance. The prince mythology can only stay in place if she blocks out the information about the quality of men's lives. She has to believe that he has a princely life.

I'm using my own life as the best example I know, but it took me a lot of work, internal work, to make myself ready to love and want to live with just a guy—just a guy who has as many life issues as I have, who's not going to save me, not going to redeem me, not going to make my life for me.

It's hard, but it's worth it.

Helen Fisher

HELEN FISHER, Ph.D., is an anthropologist at the American
Museum of Natural History in New York. She is the author of *The
Sex Contract: The Evolution of Human Behavior* and, more recently,
*Anatomy of Love: The Natural History of Monogamy, Adultery and
Divorce.*

Jack: *You mentioned on the phone that you think a book like this is
really needed. Why?*

Helen: Because there is a huge silent majority of women who are
fond of men, who have fathers they worry about, brothers they have
compassion for, husbands they support, and sons they are trying to
raise. They see men as people who need the same kind of understanding that women need. For years, if not almost a generation,
women have been grumbling about men. Has there been any other
book like this—in which women talk about what they think is
going on with men?

Not that I know of, except maybe Women Respond to the Men's
Movement. *Do you know about that?*

No. What is it?

*It's pretty nasty. It's a collection of women critiquing the men's move-
ment essentially by saying patriarchy, patriarchy, patriarchy, eighty-seven
times per chapter.*

Blamers are a personality type and they seem to have outdone themselves on this particular issue. You know, we have a lack of sophistication about history in this culture. We tend to blame men for patriarchy, when in fact it was simply caused by evolution.

In hunting-gathering societies, for millions of years, men and women were relatively equal. Women left camp in the morning to do their gathering. They commuted to work; they left their children in day care. They came home with at least fifty percent, if not seventy or eighty and sometimes one hundred percent, of the evening meal. In the past, the double income was always the norm. Men and women were built to put their heads together, there was general equality in hunting-gathering societies. Then with the beginning of plow agriculture, men and women both settled down on the farm and women lost their ancient roles as gatherers. Men's roles as farmers became much more important. Not only did men have to till the soil with heavy plows, but they had to protect the soil. So the roles of plowman and warrior became more important, and an economic imbalance between men and women emerged.

But patriarchy wasn't a plot concocted by men. It was the result of an ecological conundrum. The big animals were dying out. The smaller animals were harder and harder to hunt. The fishing spots were being taken up. With the beginning of plow agriculture some ten thousand years ago we saw the evolution of a patriarchal society among our Western ancestors, and the establishment of all kinds of new rules. But these rules were not only directed at women; they also constricted men.

Is there an analogy in modern culture between the plow diminishing women's roles and the computer diminishing men's?

There seem to be two important trends that are enabling women to return to economic equality with men. One is globalization. We're moving into an age of communication. Women are more skilled at communication then men are, on average of course, which probably comes from millions of years of living on the grasslands when women had to raise their children by talking, cajoling, reprimanding, soothing, educating their young. Women are very fine at language skills, and I think the next century is going to be built with words. Look at all the women on television and in journalism, for example. The second factor is that we're moving more and more toward entrepreneurism, the small business. Something like four out of five new businesses are started by women, not by men. The traditional kind of company is very hierarchical, but the emerging business structure, in which all kinds of free-lance, satellite people provide services and income to each other, is a very female business model in that transactions are not hierarchical but lateral instead. With the rise of service industries, women—and men—have all sorts of new opportunities.

So why aren't men also starting small businesses?

That's a good question. My guess is that there's probably not as much of a Glass Ceiling for men in traditional companies, so they have more incentive to stay.

Could it also have something to do with enthusiasm? Something about who's been hearing the pep rally for twenty years? Women have been hearing, "Yea, women! Go for it!" and men have been hearing "You're scum, you're a dog, you deserve every bad thing that ever happens to you!"

I don't know whether that's it. If more men are staying in the large companies, my guess would be that (*a*) there are more opportunities for them, (*b*) they are less likely to take a real chance, because they can't afford the risk. For millions of years women have been attracted to men with resources. Young girls like men with fancy cars or gold bracelets, middle-aged women like men with stable jobs and boats and houses, and older women like men with status, money, securities. So men are probably psychologically less willing to jeopardize a very standard job than women are. I don't think that men have the freedom to experiment. Men in every culture around the world sacrifice more time, health, happiness, and comforts in order to achieve and maintain rank than women do.

> [The] "sacrifice-to-feed" is the male form of nurturance. In every class, men with families provide their own womb, the family's financial womb. They provide their bodies. But the psychology of disposability leaves them without placards saying "my body, my choice."
>
> WARREN FARRELL, Ph.D.
> *The Myth of Male Power: Why Men Are the Disposable Sex*

What does that tell us about women's Glass Ceiling?

Oh boy. What does it tell us? Well, I don't know. Do you have an idea?

I'm thinking that most men do not rise to elevated positions in corporations and that elevated positions in corporations are not all they're cracked up to be.

Sure. You get up there and you work continually. I think that women just want that choice. They want the choice to not have the Glass Ceiling there. Men don't have a lot of choice either.

Yes, exactly. On the stock market, options are commodities that people pay money for whether they exercise them or not. Do you think that maybe women are paying a price for their options?

Their options of working? I think it's natural for women to work. It's a natural part of the human female.

I mean the option of not working. If an option is a commodity, is it not understandable that men would expect to be compensated for the options they are giving up?

I don't think that men expect a great deal, to be honest with you. I really don't. They somehow deep in their souls think they've got a pretty good deal. They even feel a little bit guilty for having such a good deal. It is strange that our society has gotten men to think that they shouldn't expect more out of life. Don't they have more heart disease? Don't they die younger? Don't they commit suicide more often?

But it's strange. When you ask people who's happy in their marriages, a lot more women say they're unhappy in marriages than men do.

It's worth pondering whether men are happy because they're married or married because they're happy. And the surveys don't necessarily tell us what's going on in the marriage. These responses could be just a reflection of what women expect and think they have a right to.

You may be right. Perhaps women expect more out of marriages than men do.

So what do you think of this constant harangue about patriarchy, patriarchy, patriarchy?

The whole question of patriarchy has gotten out of hand. Naomi Wolf came out with that ridiculous book *The Beauty Myth,* in which she basically blamed men and the entire advertising industry for the fact that women had to remain beautiful and thin all their lives. But for millions of years, men have been attracted to women who look youthful. That was an evolutionarily adaptive response on men's part because clear eyes, white teeth, smooth skin, a youthful appearance indicated that the woman was more likely to have fresher eggs and more likely to bear more viable young. As a result, men forever have been attracted to women who look healthy and young. If the New York City advertising, cosmetic and clothing industries fell into the Hudson River tomorrow morning, women would re-create them, because the female human animal instinctively seeks to look youthful, healthy and attractive. Now *that* has nothing to do with patriarchy.

What do you think of what's being said these days about matriarchy?

If we're defining matriarchy as "female rule," there's never been such a thing. There's no archaeological evidence of one. There's no question that there are living cultures in which there are female goddesses, fertility cults and so on. But even in those societies the vast majority of ranked positions are held by men. So we have no evidence of a matriarchy anywhere in the past or anywhere on earth today.

What spawned this desire to believe in matriarchy?

My guess is that it was a feminist attempt to balance the issue of women, men and power. But even though there's never been any evidence of a matriarchy, there's a solid kernel of truth to this feminist plea: for millions of years in hunting-gathering societies there was relative equality between the sexes. Had they said *that,* instead of saying that we came from a primitive matriarchy, they would have been correct.

I want to suggest that what you just said about the feminists being partially right is also partially wrong . . .

Oh, it's quite wrong.

But for a different reason. Even societies which would by classical, androcentric definitions of power be thought of as egalitarian weren't necessarily actually egalitarian, because there has been no analysis applied to the noneconomic resources that were largely controlled by women. When we talk about equality between the sexes, we only talk about making sure women have equal shares of what men have. We are not yet talking about men having as much of what women have. And I think that's going to be the really hard part in our move toward gender equality.

There's no question that there are all kinds of things that women have that men deserve too, like more time with their children and less pressure to succeed in the material world. We need to begin to appreciate the sacrifices men make at work in order to be good husbands and good fathers. Women's sexual and reproductive resources are enormous and men expend a great deal of effort to gain access to them. Women are the custodians of the egg and it's men who flutter around women in order to reproduce themselves.

It's not just the egg. The guys who are paying prostitutes for sex or having affairs have no interest in the egg.

No. They are looking for sex, friendship, excitement, affection—a vast array of psychological comforts. But millions of years ago, those males who sought sex had more children, passing along to modern men their interest in sex and all the psychological benefits they acquire from women's worlds.

So there's affection?

Of course. Men love affection.

Acceptance?

Acceptance is very important to men.

And as you mentioned, relationships with the children are something men want to have.

Absolutely. That's one reason why divorce is so difficult for men.

Would it be a good idea to ask women to acknowledge that they've got these resources?

Yes, I think that women should recognize the incredible power of their sexuality. In fact this is one of the problems with sexual harassment. I feel very sorry for men. Women say, for example, "I have the right to wear anything I want to the office."

But they do have that right.

They do have the right, there's no question about it. But in the mating game they should know that there are consequences to wearing a blouse that is scooped down to your nipples and a skirt that is up to your fanny. Men respond to this. They respond *naturally*. We've got men absolutely terrified in the office. They don't know how to behave anymore. And they don't know how to behave because the sexes see sexual harassment so differently and both men and women need to be educated into what the other honestly considers sexual harassment. We have to show women how *not* to smile. How *not* to touch. You can't go casually grazing a man on the elbow and asking him what he thinks of the memo you wrote. You can't touch him like that. You can't walk in and starting sucking on the tip of your pencil. And you can't go and lean over his shoulder and let your hair flop against his cheek. Actually, you can. Our society certainly permits women to do that. But as an anthropologist I know there's something much more primitive going on called the human mating game. In fact, we probably weren't designed to work together at all. Women were designed to go off gathering and men were designed to go off hunting and we were probably designed primarily to pick each other up and to flirt with each other. So men respond to all kinds of subtle cues that women give off—all of their makeup, all of their cosmetic smells, the way their dresses swish, their high-heeled shoes, all kinds of things. And then women wonder why men aren't respecting the rules. Basically, the rules have not been defined. And neither men nor women understand what's going on.

Do you have any idea of what goes on in sexual-harassment sensitivity training at corporations?

No. I don't. And I need to know.

Do you suspect that it's balanced?

I doubt it, because sexual harassment is an issue that unfortunately has been controlled by women. I feel very strongly about this: we have to educate not only men but we have to educate women into the kinds of signals they are sending off.

It's interesting: it reminds me of a business situation that a colleague told me about recently. It was a very hot summer day in a crowded meeting room. A man was seated behind a woman. Suddenly, she leaned back and swept her hair up onto her head and then tossed her hair out, just, I guess, because she was too hot. Immediately, the man sitting behind her looked at my colleague, who was next to him, and said, "She wants me." Now, this sounds absurd. But she had probably sent at least two signals. Perhaps he had received her smell. Moreover, the "head toss" is a primitive gesture. Horses do it, birds do it. And women do it. This man picked up a primal courting cue. Should the woman have not tossed her hair? I believe in freedom. Of course she should have the option to toss her hair. But she should *know* the signals that she is sending . . .

And the man should also know.

And the man should begin to realize that he has responded to a primitive signal, but he has to respect her ignorance and not take this as a come-on. The mating game is powerful and primitive. It's not going to go away. And if we don't respect it, we're going to continue to misunderstand each other on a very basic level.

There's a great deal that both sexes need to learn about that. But unfortunately right now all the blame is on men.

What would you say to women who are going to object that you are placing restrictions, you're just like men, trying to control women's choices?

I would say that very deep in the human spirit are ancient evolutionary drives, and if we don't respect them, we aren't going to have good will toward men *or* women.

Now, just for the record, are you blaming women for their behavior in the office?

No. I'm interested in educating women. And I'm interested in educating men. There's this big biological dance and we don't have our steps down. We don't get it. Neither of the sexes gets it.

Do you see any connection between the issues we're talking about and social problems other than the obvious ones like sexual harassment?

Well, we've got some real social problems, like drug abuse. That's a real social problem.

Do you see a connection between these gender issues and drug abuse, crime, teenage pregnancy?

We've got a great problem in our inner cities because a great many women move into business and men move into drugs and into jail and die.

Is that because men are naturally more inclined to break laws?

No, it's because many inner-city ghetto men don't seem to have the same opportunities that women do. They don't achieve their basic role as providers, so they turn to drugs and crime in frustration and die out.

Since in the past thirty years we have taken from men the exclusive province of being providers, would it be wise for us as a society that's concerned about men and crime to open up options for men, other than options that require them to have money?

Absolutely.

Do you have any thoughts about what those options might be from an anthropological perspective?

Oh boy. It would be great if we had larger numbers of older men playing more nurturing roles to get young men going. But once again the problem is that the genders tend to have different interests. We're not alike. Even if we opened up enormous opportunities for men in day care I doubt that men would go for it.

Men wouldn't want to do it in day care. That's a woman's thing. Women have day care where they all sit in one place and they all do the sedentary things. A male style of day care would probably require four acres.

Right. And it would be very good for children. I'm making a speech to a country day school about whether we should see gender as a resource.

I wonder if the school uses terms like class mother. *And I wonder if they schedule their parent meetings at three o'clock in the afternoon.*

Right. You have pinpointed yet another legacy of our patriarchal past. For a long time it was women who were at home and women who had that domain. But things are changing.

What about other social problems?

There certainly is a family form in America that is totally matrilineal. Women get their government checks and the community is largely female-oriented. Males do not play an important role in family life. There's no question about it.

From an anthropological point of view, what's likely or maybe even inevitable to happen in that circumstance?

We're seeing it happen. The men get their esteem and their money by selling drugs and robbing and end up in jail and dying. It's incredible the percentage of men in the underclass that can't get into the mainstream, can't get the resources of society, so they take alternative routes and die out.

We've got a lot to learn. But I'll say this. It has been said that men want to be needed and women want to be cherished. Men's desire to be needed comes from millions of years ago when our ancestors evolved the human drive to pair up and raise their children as a team. If we can make men feel needed *and* cherished, we'll come a long way toward ending the war between the sexes.

Doris Caldwell

DORIS CALDWELL is a registered nurse working in alcohol-
and drug-abuse treatment for the De Kalb County health department
in Atlanta, Georgia. She is a member of the U.S. Army Nurse
Corps at Fort Benning, Georgia, and in that capacity has worked as
a psychiatric nurse in substance-abuse programs at American military
posts in Germany. Doris also volunteers as an adviser to the National Black Men's Health Network. She is married, has one grown
son and was born in 1948.

Jack: *I understand that you want to talk specifically about what's
happening with African-American men.*

Doris: Yes. I see a lot of African-American men not being involved in their children's lives. I hear a lot of men complaining that
when a couple breaks up, it's automatic that the woman gets the
child, whether he likes it or not.

These are men in substance-abuse programs?

Yes. They have to fight for their rights to be parents to their
children. That's a big issue for them, whereas for the women, it's
just understood that they are going to be the ones who get custody
of the children.

*Are these men suggesting that the problem they're having with sub-
stance abuse is a result of losing their place in the family?*

A lot of them are involved in substance abuse first. But a lot of them aren't. They develop the substance-abuse problem after their lives have been torn apart, whether it's divorce, or the children going to the wife, loss of job, loss of self-respect, different things that cause them a lot of pain. They turn to the substance to medicate the pain they're feeling over being no longer in control of their lives.

Can you give me some idea of the kind of pain these men are expressing about not being allowed to be parents?

Last week, for example, some of the men were talking about the child support enforcement agency, which in Atlanta is called Child Support Recovery. One man talked about how he and his wife had separated. After he lost his job, there was no longer love between them. They both loved their children; they just no longer loved each other. When they separated, the wife took the kids out of the home, went back to her parents, and he was left by himself. He was feeling pain over wondering how he could get back into the children's lives and be a worthwhile citizen again. He was looking for work, but since he had no job, he felt like he had nothing to offer the mother, other than his love for the children, and that didn't seem to be enough. That's when Child Support Recovery got involved, and threw him in jail. He just kept bouncing from jail to street; he never could get ahead. And he wasn't able to see the children at all. He verbalized a lot of pain about that. Naturally, when he went to court to try to get custody, the first thing they asked was "How would you support these kids?" He had no income, so the judge said the kids were better off with the mother.

:   Some of the procedures used by [child-support enforcement] agen-
:   cies in their dealings with young unwed fathers and mothers have
:   created a perception of these agencies as hostile and punitive to
:   fathers.
:
:
:   JACQUELINE SMOLLAR, Ph.D., AND
:   THEODORA OOMS, MSW
:   "Young Unwed Fathers: Research Review, Policy
:   Dilemmas and Options"
:   funded by the Department of Health and
:   Human Services
:   October 1987

Did the judge ask her *how* she *would support the kids?*

The man said that never came up; it was automatically under-stood in the court hearing that he was the one who should provide for the family. If he couldn't do that, she could get public assistance without him.

And why was it not thought that he should be the one to get public assistance and keep the kids?

He never applied for public assistance. When we asked him, he said, "No, men just don't do that." I don't know if it's a family thing, or honor, but he never even thought of applying for it.

Is it common when a man loses his job for the woman to think he's no good anymore?

Very common. I see it all the time.

What do you think of this woman's idea that the only thing the man was good for, the only thing his family needed from him, was his money?

It wasn't just the woman who was thinking this; the man was thinking it, too. It's in your upbringing. We have always said that the man is the head of the household. It's almost a religious thing: if you're a man, you provide for your family. And I think that's what he was basing some of his thinking on, that made him feel so worthless.

Contrary to prevailing stereotypes, the [noncustodial fathers] in these focus groups [in Harlem] expressed powerful feelings about men's responsibilities toward their families. . . . Much of the discussion in these groups dealt with the fact that many of these men have difficulty supporting even themselves.

MERCER L. SULLIVAN
"Noncustodial Fathers' Attitudes and Behaviors"
Caring and Paying: What Fathers and Mothers Say About Child Support
Manpower Demonstration Research Corporation
July 1992

I get the impression that if an African-American man can't produce economically, he's not considered good for much of anything.

It's a strong idea that the male should be the one who brings the funds in. And I have to admit that I'm not sure that, deep down, I don't really feel the same way, too. But working with these men, and seeing how they feel about their children, I have a different view. I know that even though the men are supposedly macho, even though they're not looked upon as the ones who nurture kids, they truly *do* nurture their kids, they want to be a part of their kids' lives, and they lose part of themselves when they lose their kids. They want to be the person who goes to the first day of school, who goes to the PTA, who goes to the counselor's office and says, "Okay, tell me what's going on with my child," just as the mother would. And I see the pain that they go through when the children are not in their lives, and how they wish they could be there for the birthdays, for the first tooth that comes out, the little things that you normally didn't think a male focuses on. You just don't think a man is capable of loving the way a mother is, but he is. I'm beginning to see that. I see it all differently today.

What did you think before you started working with these guys?

I thought that maybe the man just wasn't trying hard enough, and even though he lost that job, he still should have been a survivor and should have had something to fall back on, since he was a male. There again it's that stereotype that the male is the one who should bring the income to the family. That's how I was reared.

What do these fellows say to you in counseling? What words do you hear?

I see a lot of tears. That's different for me. To see a male cry today is something that I thought I would never see. But you actually see tears; you actually see them go through a lot of stress, a lot of heartache. Normally you would say, "Oh, he's a male; surely he wouldn't cry." But I see this. I see them cry. I see the tears.

Are we talking about individual counseling? Group counseling?

Group counseling and individual. And to see a male cry in a group says to me, "He is hurting."

Are these African-American and white groups together?

Yes, it's a mixed group. You see the pain with both, the white and the black.

Generally, do you see any differences between the way African-American men and white men react in these situations?

Not a whole lot, but the white males tend to have more family support, and they may have funds from an inheritance or from a family member who can afford to help them, as opposed to the black male, who may not have that kind of support. You see some differences there. But sometimes it's vice versa.

If you were to go to talk to a judge, what would you say on behalf of these guys?

I think they should have shared custody. I think the woman should have six months in that child's life, then the male six months. Or every other week. I think it should be shared, providing that he has a place to take the children.

If I'm the judge and I say, "I'm interested in what's best for the child," what are you going to tell me about why it's best for the child to have the man in the child's life?

It's important for the child to know that the father still loves him or her and that the problem is just situational stuff, like no income, that the father is having a problem with his self-esteem in not being able to provide for his family. I would just say to the judge, "If at all possible, don't throw him in jail for having no funds. Give him a chance to get a new career, to help try to put this family back together." Now if this person was not trying, if he has abandoned the family, that's a different story. But if this father is really wanting to be in his child's life, and really wants to get back in society by finding a new career, or a new job, I think we should give him that chance.

When you say that the father is trying to put the family together, what can he do to put the family back together?

Get employed. Get a home for the family, an apartment or something. Put them back under the same roof. Learn how to get along with them.

Are you telling me that if a guy gets a job, his wife is more likely to find him lovable?

Acceptable.

Acceptable.

Yes. That he is trying to provide for their family. And that he's not just goofing off, that he's not out of work just because he doesn't want to work.

Let's suppose the guy got laid off, he's trying to find a job, but he can't find one. The woman knows he's trying. Is she any less likely, knowing that he's trying to find a job, to want to split from him?

Some families are like that; some are not. Some women, with the belief that he should be the provider, may not accept him being laid off, even though she knows the economy is in a mess and people are not finding jobs right away. The anger of having the burden of raising these children doesn't stop, so her anger may kick in, and she'll say, "Well, wait a minute, I've got to have an income. No matter how, you've got to do it. You've got to bring some money in." That's what we hear a lot of times. Even though the woman knows that he has no job, and that people are just not hiring right now, she still has the anger and all the frustration of providing for the child. So I think sometimes with the anger that they feel, they aren't always rational about the situation. It's "I want you to do it and I want you to do it now."

And if you don't do it now, if you don't find a job now, I don't need you?

Right.

And the kids don't need you?

Right.

Are they trying to punish the guy?

I don't think it's punishment, I think it's situational stress. They just can't cope with not having that money. You know how you lose common sense sometimes when you're angry?

What good does it do her to get rid of the guy?

It doesn't do any good, but yet we see these situations. If he gets her involved in counseling, it helps. It helps her understand that he's going through a difficult time, that he's really trying to help.

Even though he doesn't have a job, he still wants to be a part of the family life. Usually when they start talking, it gets better.

What kind of things need to be said?

What jobs, what interviews he's going out to. How often is he going? How much is he really trying to get that job?

Does the woman think she's feeling more stress than he's feeling?

I think so. Because the children are with her.

But she took the children.

Right. But I don't think she reasoned that part, because society says the children belong with the woman. I think she takes that burden simply because she's the mother, and she feels that those kids must stay with her, no matter what.

Is the whole idea of the man, then, to help her raise the kids? He is to be her assistant?

They never really focus in on it that way, but deep down, that's truly what it is, even though they may deny it when you ask them.

If a woman doesn't have a job, or if she loses her job, does she lose her self-esteem in the family?

No, we accept that. We accept that readily, that a woman doesn't have to have a job, even though a lot of them do. She doesn't necessarily have to be a breadwinner.

What's special about her?

We assume that she is the one who nurtures and takes care of the children, and makes most of the decisions for the child. I don't think there's anything special; it's just that society gives her that role.

If society gave men that role . . .

Then we would see a different family function. You would see a family who may look upon the male in a different light. Yes, he's there to nurture just like the woman. Yes, he should have custody just like the woman. But it's not like that yet. If I separated from my husband when my child was smaller, my family would have expected me to bring my child home to them. If I had given my child to my husband, I would have been viewed as the bad guy there. You know: "How dare you give your child to this man?"

Even if you really thought he'd be the better parent?

Right. Even though he was a counselor, he was a schoolteacher, he was a leader in the community, I think my family still would have had a problem with me giving my child to him.

What's so horrible about a man raising a child?

I just don't think society has given men the opportunity. He was never assigned to nurture the child. That's just the way our society is made up, that the children stay with the mother. We accept that; that's the way it's always been.

What percentage of the men you see really want to find a job, and what percentage do you think are not really interested?

I think only about two percent are not really interested. The rest, I think, are truly interested in a job, a real job, and improving their skills and getting a job that has meaning, giving them back a power base, to make some decisions in the world.

If the Clinton administration could generate five hundred thousand new jobs tomorrow, that would be great. But it's probably not going to happen. What would you think of a program that helped these guys feel that being a father was an important job, and that kept them from losing that job?

That would be wonderful. If we could help the father learn—even if he's only learning what his child is learning in school today—I think you would see a better citizen, because a lot of times when we interview these males, you find that the basis of their low self-esteem is that they just don't understand reading, writing, and arithmetic. After we started a GED* program in our building, you saw these men increase their self-esteem. They can go home and read to the child, and understand what the child is doing in school, and help teach the child. They're much happier. That would be a wonderful program. The long-range goal would be to get them employed, but until they're employed, they could improve their outlook, their feeling of self-worth by being fathers and teachers to

* General Educational Development test, an alternative means of gaining a high school diploma

their children. I think that would make a difference. You wouldn't
see as much anger about being a failure, as much anger in general.
It might even reduce the crime rate.

That's what I'm thinking.

*When it comes to paying child support, do you ever hear these guys
talk about the fact that their money doesn't really go to their kids, that
except for $50 per month, it just goes to pay the government back for
welfare?*

Yes, you hear that.

The [noncustodial fathers in focus groups in Harlem] were keenly
aware that payments to children on AFDC [Aid to Families with
Dependent Children] do relatively little to improve the children's
welfare. Thus, efforts to explain the $50 "disregard" (money passed
through from child support payments by noncustodial parents to
custodial parents on AFDC) might help, and expanding it might
help even more.

MERCER L. SULLIVAN
"Noncustodial Fathers' Attitudes and Behaviors"
*Caring and Paying: What Fathers and Mothers Say
About Child Support*
Manpower Demonstration Research Corporation
July 1992

*What do you think that does to the motivation of the guy who's
supposed to be paying this money?*

If his money isn't going to his kids, I don't think he's going to
pay it.

What needs to happen to make this situation better?

We need to start looking at the male as someone who belongs in
a family, that the male is just as important as the female in nurturing a child, that the male should make decisions for his child,
and that he should be given joint custody of his child. Once we
start doing that, society will begin to look at our males in a different
light. His family values are basically the same as everybody else's.

Laurie Ingraham

LAURIE INGRAHAM, MSW, is the director and owner of the Addictive Relationships Center in Brookfield, Wisconsin, a suburb of Milwaukee. She has been a psychotherapist since 1983 and specializes in addictions—alcohol, drugs, food, work, gambling, and especially relationships. She has worked with women's issues throughout her psychotherapeutic career and since 1988 has focused on men's issues. In 1992 she began organizing the Women's International Network for Healthy Relationships. She is writing a book whose working title is *Men and Women: You Can't Live With Them and You Can't Live Without Them.*

Jack: *Do you think sexism against men is a serious problem?*

Laurie: Absolutely. The women's movement needed to happen, but it went to an extreme of saying that the only way women can become empowered is by putting men down.

Did prejudices against men exist before the women's movement, or are they only a product of the women's movement?

No, they've been around for a long time.

What's making it worse today?

Competition. "We're better than you are; you're worse than we are." Competition is destructive in relationships.

They say we're in the Year of the Woman. I believe that the intention of a lot of women is to say men have fucked up the world and that women should be in control. There's a strong undertone of moral superiority to women's competitiveness.

I believe that women are the more spiritually advanced sex.

ERICA JONG
Washington Post
December 6, 1992

What are men's supposed moral inferiorities?

Men are cold, calculating, unfeeling, inconsiderate, rude, self-ish, those kinds of things. Basically, by the age of three, our parents, TV and movies have taught us not to trust you.

Women also pick up a lot of biases by observing their mothers. Many women saw that their mothers were unhappy in their marriages and they saw one of two basic behaviors from the mother. At one extreme the mother directly tells the daughters, "Men are horrible; don't ever trust them; they're just going to hurt you. Men are bad. Your father stinks." But at the other extreme the mother is covert and passive and caters to the father, and says, "Well, your father needs this; your father needs that," but lets the daughter know she isn't happy about it. And in both extremes the mother and daughter align with each other. The message is that everybody has to tolerate this male person. That's a big source of prejudices.

But it gets worse. Imagine being raised as a young Ku Klux Klan member, someone who has been raised to hate African-Americans. Then, as you enter adolescence, you are told to start dating African-Americans and eventually you must marry one. It's insane, but that's what women are told about men: you are to be scared and prejudiced and afraid of men and think that they're going to hurt you and leave you, but ignore all those feelings and go out and find one to marry anyway.

It takes a lot of work to get past those prejudices. Now any Ku Klux Klan member could easily find black Americans who would fulfill his prejudices. He could say, "I'm right. Look at this guy, look at this guy." And any woman who holds prejudices against men can always find proof. So they have to be determined to prove themselves wrong. And not too many people like to do that.

What do women have invested in their prejudices against men?

It keeps them safe. As long as they can believe their biases, they don't have to take risks, they don't have to take responsibility for their lives. They have the perfect reason to stay the same.

It seems that sex also has a lot to do with women's distrust of men.

And with men's distrust of women. Women learn that if they're not sexual, they could be rejected. And they feel a real fear of abandonment. But they also find out that a guy will do anything to get laid. And that's pretty powerful; they control whether that man's going to get laid.

For a woman's sexual power to be in place, is it necessary for her to be someone men want to have sex with, someone men think about having sex with?

Definitely.

So the power of sexuality requires getting right up to the edge of desirability and availability, but when a woman falls or gets bumped or pulled over the edge, it's typically seen as the man's fault.

That's true. And she shames him royally for it.

Does this tell us anything about sexual harassment?

Women need to take responsibility for saying no. They also need to not smile and be coy as if they don't mind a flirtatious comment when they really do. If you don't want to have sex with a man, then don't come on as being sexually interested, giving signals that you would like to be pursued. And if women don't like what's going on around them, they should say they don't like it. But women often don't deal with things up front; they go and talk to their girlfriends about something a guy did and they say, "Ooh, that's sexual harassment." Oh, do you think so? "Oh, yeah, that's sexual harassment." Most people, women and men, are immature emotionally, but a lot of women in this regard are functioning at around age nine or ten. They are afraid to confront another person, especially a male, adult-to-adult. They will often act like everyone around them is a big, powerful parent and they are victims. Unless women truly grow up and access their adulthood, harassment merely says, "This mean person is bothering me and I'm powerless to stop it." It's like the little kid in the sandbox. Johnny steals her toy and she cries, "Mommy, Mommy, Johnny stole my toy." And instead of Mommy saying, "Well, grab it back and tell him to knock it off," Mommy slaps Johnny and says, "Don't you take my daughter's toy."

Would it be too callous to say to women, "If you don't want to get burned sexually, don't play with fire?"

No, it wouldn't be too callous to say.

Do women play with fire?

They do. Women want to be sexual and be desired by men, but not feel like they invited it, because of guilt messages from childhood.

They want to be hot, but they don't want to get burned?

Right. I've been in groups where women have owned it openly that they really get off on being hot. In a group in California an attractive young woman said, "I've done that to men millions of times; it feels good to know that they're panting after me, and I just have to go like this with my finger. That gives me great pleasure." One of the men in the group got up and screamed at her, "Goddamn you fucking bitch! I have been hurt by women like you so many goddamn times." And that's how women rape men. If you don't want to be sexual with a man, do not put out sexual messages. That's all there is to it.

> I have a friend whose hobby is corresponding with guys who are away at college or in the service. She writes duplicate love letters and encloses locks of hair. . . . Rose says it "amuses" her to receive their responses filled with passion and declarations of undying love.
>
> Eddie in the Bronx
> writing to *Dear Abby*
> *Baltimore Sun*
> March 11, 1990

We talked about relationships in which the wife is not happy with the husband. Would you expect that despite her unhappiness with him, he's very happy with her?

Men tend to be much more tolerant of women in a lot of ways; they distance off and don't want to deal with the problems.

So the way he's dealing with it is not very healthy either, is it?

No. Often, men like to please women and gain their approval, so they give their power away. Men are incredibly afraid of women; they have tremendous fear of women if they feel that the woman is going to criticize them. Frequently when he expresses himself, she says, "Oh, don't be so ridiculous; I can't believe you're saying that!" or "Why don't you ever talk about your feelings?" Then when the guy talks about his feelings, she'll often say, "That's stupid!" or "You can't really feel that way!" So the way he sees it is never right. And so the guy shuts down, and he refuses to talk. That's what I see in my practice over and over. The guy wonders, "Why should I open my mouth, when every time I do, she tells me it's wrong?"

What's really sad is that a lot of men who were raised in the sixties and seventies in the middle of the women's movement can connect with women only by totally seeing the woman's side. I've done conferences at universities where the men are scared to death to even consider that they have a side, because the women and the women's studies programs are totally dominant. Many young men are coming out of universities saying, "Yeah, men are assholes." As young boys, they saw their mothers being unhappy with their fathers, and, as adolescents, heard their girlfriends tell story after story of men hurting or victimizing them. So a lot of men are busy paying off their debt to society through sympathizing with women when they weren't the violators. I see a lot of that going on. The "in thing" is to totally support women no matter what.

: I felt guilty. No, it wasn't my fault. . . . Somehow I still felt
: guilty. My guilt was not just because I felt helpless, but also because

I belonged to that group called "men" who seemed always to be at
the root of the problem.

PETE R.,
upon hearing a woman talk about being raped
"A Guy's Perspective on Rape"
The Listener, April 1991
Loyola College, Baltimore

*It almost seems like Coke versus Pepsi, men versus women. Which
one's more cool than the other?*

Right.

Right now women are much more cool than men.

That's it.

*And if you side with men, you're obviously a nerd. A sociological
nerd.*

[It is] fashionably American [to] regard the father as insignificant,
ridiculous, absurd. . . . Something in the culture wants us to be
unfair to our father's masculine side . . . assume he is a monster, as
some people say all men are.

ROBERT BLY
Iron John

This is so true. I tell women this: If you want to change how men
deal with you and how you deal with them, then you must quit
criticizing what they say, and listen to what they say. Just listen.
The typical thing that happens is that a man will say something,
and the woman will say, "Hah! That's what a man would think!"
A few years ago, I was at a Christmas party. A woman began
talking about her husband and how stupid he was for not being able
to do a simple mechanical job at home. She went on to say how all
men are like that and how women really have to put up with a lot

from men's inconsistencies and it's amazing we have survived them. The women laughed and the men smiled and nodded or shrugged. No one objected or seemed to be offended. One man got up, supposedly to get some coffee, and came into the kitchen and said to me, "I am so sick of parties where the majority of the conversation is about how men are screwed up and make all the mistakes in the world." I asked him why he didn't speak up, and he said he had tried once and all the women rolled their eyes and got on his case. He said, "No wonder men just sit there and don't say anything. If you speak up, you hear about it at home about how you ruined the party and 'women don't mean anything by it,' so we just take it."

It's amazing to me that in groups of men and women in public places the men will start talking about very interesting neutral subjects, and the women will start in on them with their little female-bonding comments that disparage men. And everyone laughs, ha-ha-ha-ha-ha.

Are the men and women both laughing about the same thing? And in the same way?

The women are laughing harder. The men are smiling and staying silent. Because they don't dare say, "Hey, I didn't appreciate that comment."

Why not?

They almost never do.

Why not?

They're petrified.

Why?

They're scared of women and what women think of them.

Why?

It goes back to mommy stuff. Men are not ever to say anything to upset their mothers, ever. The guilt is too tremendous. It used to be that men spoke up, but the women's movement changed that. We're seeing female-dominated males who are so afraid of offending women that they will sit in a room and be ridiculed; it doesn't even occur to them to say boo.

Does this just roll off men like water off a duck, or . . .

They're affected. You can see them squirm.

So they squirm. Is that the end of it?

Yep.

You don't think men are harboring any anger or resentment?

I think they're used to it. I think they're building armor against it; it's just conditioning.

Does this conditioning lead to a general demeaning of what women have to say, as in "I don't pay any attention to them"?

Yes. They'll blow women off. Or if they go into rebellion you'll hear, "I'm sick of that goddamn shit. You're always trying to push your stuff on me, and I'm so goddamn sick of this!" Boom! He'll go into the dominant male role: "I'm going to put you in your fucking place!"

Let's say we've got a man who is thirty minutes away from rebelling into the dominant male mode and putting the goddamn woman in her fucking place. What would you suggest to him in the interim?

At the time that a woman is ridiculing the man, he must say, "I really don't appreciate what's going on here. I don't appreciate your comment." You don't have to be mean, you don't have to be vicious, but you've got to speak up.

Just that simple?

Just that simple. But the woman will almost always respond by saying the man is unreasonable. He needs to be prepared that the woman will say, "Oh, don't be ridiculous, as if men haven't been putting us down for years." And he will not win. But the intention is not to win. The intention is to not let it go by.

So the woman snaps back. Does he need to say anything in response to her response, or can he just let it go with his first statement?

He can say, "I still don't appreciate it." That's speaking from himself. He didn't let it go by. He's not trying to change the woman, or investing in changing her, but he didn't get violated. He stood his ground.

I've even seen the problem among psychotherapists, who should know better. Three women were running a meeting of eighty or a hundred therapists in Wisconsin. One of the women was a very influential marriage and family counselor in the state, one was a social work professor at the University of Wisconsin, and the other was a Ph.D. in counseling. They started the meeting by explaining the problem: "Originally we had men on the board and, of course, that was totally inefficient, so once we got the men off the board everything was fine," and the whole room laughed. Then they implied that there had been disagreement among some of the men and that if men would just learn to stay out of the way, the problem would have been solved a lot quicker. And they all laughed again. They went on with three or four comments like this. I was getting really angry. The male colleague I was with, who is very aware of men's issues, was getting angry too, and we were writing notes back and forth, "Do we stand up now and complain, or do we wait until after?" All the other men in the room, psychologists, at least thirty of them, are just sitting there, just sitting there.

The women went on about all they'd accomplished, and really downing men in the process. At the end my male colleague went up to the front table and said, "I just want to say I really did not like the comments you made about men, and I thought they were really inappropriate, especially from professionals." And, of course, the woman said, "Well, if you're going to be so sensitive about it, it was just meant as a joke." This is a Ph.D. in counseling! And he said, "I didn't think it was funny, and I think it was really inappropriate." And she said, "Well, it wasn't meant to offend, and if it offended you, I'm sorry. Obviously, you took it wrong." And he said, "I just needed to speak my piece and tell you what I thought." And he walked away. I was at the table at the same time. The woman turned to another woman, a participant, not even one of her co-leaders, and—this is so typical—said, "What that man deserved was a 'fuck you'." And they both laughed. And I said, "Excuse me. You better read this." And I had written a long note, speaking as a professional psychotherapist, saying that I was very offended by what went on, I was shocked that women in that position would be so biased against men, especially since they are involved in counseling and therapy for couples.

And outside the room, a man came up to my colleague and said, "I heard what you said to her, and I really thank you for that, because I was feeling it but I wouldn't say it." And he said, "Why not?" And the man said, "In a room full of women? Are you kidding?" That's a perfect example of what happens. That is just so sad to me. Men need to confront this stuff. Women also need to confront it. Any time people start bad-mouthing men, you need to stand up and say, "Hey, let's knock this off."

It's frightening to think counselors, therapists could be so demeaning of men. If a man goes to couples counseling with a woman, should he be aware of the possibility that he is going to be under the guidance of a person with unhealthy attitudes toward men?

It's very, very possible. Unless a woman has truly worked her prejudices out, it's going to affect her work. And male therapists aren't necessarily going to be helpful either, because many men, especially in social work, are going to take the female's side.

How can the couple—let's assume that the woman also wants to have a balanced counseling experience—how can the couple assure themselves that they're going to be dealing with a balanced therapist?

Make sure the therapist asks both people every question, that the therapist listens to both sides. The couple can ask, "Have you worked in men's issues? Have you gone to a men's conference? Do you read men's newsletters? Have you read books about men's issues?" If the therapist answers no to all that, I would have questions about whether that therapist has a real understanding of what has to happen for the guy.

The media portrayal of men's conferences is—well go ahead, you laughed—what's the image you've picked up from the media?

Oh, drum-pounding, airy-fairy dudes running around in their underwear. And there is some of that, definitely, in some organizations. There are many facets to the men's movement. But it still gives men a place to meet other men and say, "We're not bad." If it can give them that, I don't care if they fly underwear on flagpoles, I think that's a plus.

Karen DeCrow

KAREN DECROW was president of the National Organization for Women from 1974 to 1977. She is a constitutional attorney and a coauthor, with Robert Seidenberg, of *Women Who Marry Houses: Panic and Protest in Agoraphobia.* She was born in 1937, is single, has been married twice and has no children. She lives near Syracuse, New York.

Jack: *In public buildings across the nation, there are now diaper-changing facilities for men who want to take care of their babies. You played a major role in that. How and why were you involved in making these facilities available?*

Karen: In late 1983 I was at the National Gallery in Washington, D.C. I had just come out of the women's room, where there's a whole nursery, when I saw a nice young man changing his child's diaper on the floor. I had never really thought about it before, but I went up to him and said, "You know, you have a federal case, because this is a public facility and there's a wonderful changing room for women," and then I just went off and looked at paintings.

What did the guy say to you?

I think he had a mouthful of safety pins. I had no conversation with him that I recall. But then I wrote a newspaper column on the subject for Father's Day 1984. Then the Fathers' Rights Association of New York State approached me and said they wanted to bring a lawsuit. At first we did a survey; the men's movement sort of spread its tentacles, and we canvassed facilities all over the place. We concluded that changing facilities did not exist in men's rooms and yet they did exist in women's rooms. So we brought the lawsuit in federal court in Syracuse against the city of Syracuse and the local Department of Aviation. It never went to trial, because in pretrial motions the judge indicated he was going to find in our favor. I'm condensing the legal details. At any rate, the city agreed to our demand.

We gave the city a choice of having a gender neutral changing room or simply putting in equal facilities for men wherever they existed for women. My personal choice is always gender neutral facilities, but the alternative is clearly legal. In the Syracuse airport right now, as a result of the lawsuit, there is a gender neutral changing room. The airport administration added a big sign that said, "This is a changing facility for mothers and fathers." We urged them to put it in alphabetical order, "for fathers and mothers." That sign is still there to this day. We also have a new wing in the airport, and in every men's room there's a facility equivalent to what's in the women's room.

We held a press conference that attracted over a dozen media outlets. We had not only one of the plaintiffs changing his child, but the lawyer who had represented the city in the lawsuit had become a parent. His baby was about eleven months at the time, and he was changing his baby, too. We had two men at two different tables, former adversaries, simultaneously changing their babies. Everybody was happy.

This is pretty obvious, but why was this good for the men involved?

It turned out to be good for men all over the country, because no one would have to spread out a blanket on a wet, dirty floor, to change his kid, because in an activity that they clearly participated in, i.e., traveling with children, men now were treated as equal citizens. It was good for women because, prior to the lawsuit, anytime a man and a woman were traveling with an infant, the woman would always have the responsibility of changing the child. What woman would expect her husband to put a kid down on a wet floor if she had a nice nursery? And it was beneficial to children because they would notice their fathers were full participants as parents.

There's a larger issue involved here.

Much larger.

Can you lay it out for us?

A lot of newspapers were writing humorous stories about the lawsuit, but actually it had very significant, wider implications. In our entire culture, we assume that parenting is to be done by women. This case involved the traveling public, but more significant is the whole employment situation. I've been on this campaign now for twenty-five years: anytime we talk about mothers in the work force, anytime we're talking about provisions for babies and children, time off, et cetera, we have to think about fathers also.

Does this automatic assumption we have, about mothers being the ones who take care of children, have anything to do with women's difficulties in employment?

It has everything to do with women's difficulties in employment. As long as an employer thinks "Here is a woman of childbearing age," the employer will automatically think "Here we have big trouble." It makes women a suspect classification during two decades of their work lives. If flextime, part time, parental leave, accommodations for children who get sick and for baby-sitters who quit are only for women, then women will be "the mommy class," or a potential mommy class.

   [C]laims charging sex discrimination in promotion are . . . on the increase. . . .

   "Salary inequity and pregnancy discrimination are among the most common forms of sex discrimination in the workplace," according to Helen Norton of the Women's Legal Defense Fund. . . .

   "These days, companies are more aware of laws protecting pregnant employees," says [Ruth] Jones [staff attorney for the NOW Legal Defense and Education Fund]. "But instead of eliminating this type of discrimination, employers' tactics are just becoming more subtle." . . .

[E]mployers can disguise pregnancy discrimination as layoffs, downsizing, or corporate restructuring. Oftentimes, the discrimination occurs after a woman has returned to work with inferior job assignments, negative performance evaluations, or lesser job responsibilities.

CHRISTIANE N. BROWN
Good Housekeeping
March 1993

Would it be good for women, then, if the employer had no more reason to suspect the woman than the man?

It would be essential for women that the employer not be suspicious. We shouldn't think in terms of "women and children." You and I have talked most about the very real discriminations against men in our society, because I believe they're there, no question about it, but on this whole children's issue, every time I hear that a man wants to have some connection with his children, whether it's time off or a place to change diapers, or whatever, I always think, "This is great for women," because children are, in the final analysis, the major issue in women's difficulties in combining work and personal life. You can always let the laundry pile up, and if you don't have time to cook you can do takeout. But taking care of children can't be postponed; they have to be watched twenty-four hours a day for many years.

Two points I'd like to pursue here. One is that we know about men's attitudes that contribute to the idea that women's work is to take care of kids. On the other hand in that Father's Day column, you wrote about a client of yours, a divorced mother of three. You said, "She was desperate for a sitter so she could fulfill her professional responsibilities. Because of the unusual hours involved, it was difficult to find a person to fill the job. 'What about the father?' I asked. 'Is he willing to take them during those hours?' " Do you remember her response?

"That's just what he wants." Is that right?

Yes. " 'Their father?' she exclaimed. 'That's just what he wants!' "

One of the real sorrows of my life is that in the battle between the sexes, men and women will go practically to the ends of the earth in illogical, irrational ways to give each other pain. It's just amazing. I'm not a matrimonial lawyer, but I hear from friends who are. And a lot of my clients in employment cases are getting divorced, so I hear this all the time. Both men and women will do anything to cause pain to the other person. And of course a parent's relationship with the children is the best point of all, or the worst point of all, for inflicting pain, because that really will create misery.

Let me pursue another aspect of this issue. The Family and Medical Leave Act is ostensibly gender neutral, but . . .

It's not applied that way. Maybe it will be, but in my experience many, many, many employers have a policy that's written in a gender neutral way, but when people go to take advantage of the policy, males and females are treated very differently. Although the policy says "parental leave," men who apply for leave are considered not heavy hitters, are considered, if not flaky, just not serious about work. Women are not looked down upon for wanting to take time off. Of course, they may be fired. I have a lot of cases of women who took parental leave and trained their replacements, and were just told that their replacement worked out so well that they were out of a job. That happens to a lot of women. At least now, though, people are *hearing* about fathers taking leave. I thought the law was needed, but I preferred a version that was much more definitively gender neutral.

Do you think that it might be a good idea to have some type of an affirmative action program so that men get the message that it's not just legal, it's not just tolerable, but it's really okay, we really want you to take advantage of this?

Absolutely. And whether it's seminars or films—this is on a very different subject, but they could do a movie on it. That would be great. Did you see *Men Don't Tell*, the movie Sunday night about a husband who gets beaten up by his wife?

I sure did. I saw everything but the first twenty minutes.

It was fabulous that they broadcast it, because, of course, anybody who talks to men knows that family violence goes both ways, though the image is that it only goes one way. People get caught up in the statistics: is it fifty percent men or forty percent? It doesn't matter. The fact is family violence is ubiquitous and it goes both ways. So here was a movie that did well in the ratings and it made a point that people going around lecturing ten years couldn't make. Everybody saw it. And I would guess an awful lot of battered men are now thinking, "Oh my goodness, I'm not the only one; this happens."

Now you mentioned an affirmative action program. I think that kind of thing about fathers taking family leave would be great.

As I was getting ready to talk with you today, I went to the library and found an article published in the New York Times Magazine *almost exactly twenty-five years ago, March 10, 1968. It struck me that there was a time when feminism was very badly ridiculed.*

> [W]hen pink refrigerators abound, when women (51 per cent of the population) hold unparalleled consumer power, when women control most of the corporate stocks, when women have ready access to higher education and to the professions, when millions of women are gainfully employed, when all the nation is telling American women, all the time, that they are the most privileged female population on earth, the insistence on a civil-rights movement for women does seem a trifle stubborn.
>
> MARTHA WEINMAN LEAR
> the *New York Times Magazine*
> March 10, 1968

Who wrote this article?

Let's see. It was by Martha Weinman Lear.

Oh, I remember that. I remember that article.

What do you remember about it?

I remember that we were all furious about it. That's about it. (*Laughter.*) I can't even remember if she dealt with NOW, I just remember we were enraged, as we always were about everything that they wrote about us.

Do you see any similarities between the way the media treated feminism twenty-five years ago and the way the media have been treating men's effort to get their act together? I mean, the women's movement was reduced to bra-burning, and men are portrayed as doing nothing but beating drums and hugging trees.

You know, we never burned a bra.

It was just a false image? Nobody ever burned a bra?

No. Nobody ever burned a bra. And we were called bra-burners. In other words, someone invented that, presumably as an image that would terrify everyone. I'll tell you how it started. I was there. Do you remember when there was a demonstration in front of the Miss America Pageant?

Yes. In Atlantic City?

Right. We had something we called the Freedom Trash Can— our media images were kind of sweet and innocent in those days— one of these metal cans that they have on the boardwalk. We threw into the Freedom Trash Can artifacts that we felt oppressed women and then we were going to burn them. Most of the artifacts had to do with so-called glamour stuff because we were protesting the Miss America Pageant. Some of us brought hair spray and curlers, and makeup, lipstick. Somebody brought pages from *Vogue* that showed women as vacuous models—and somebody brought a bra, as being uncomfortable or whatever. We were going to burn this stuff, but the cops told us that if we had a fire, the aerosol hair spray would be dangerous, it could explode. So, militants that we were, we said, "Well, then we won't have a fire, we'll just have a trash can." If we had burned the contents of that trash can, a bra might have been included, because somebody did bring a bra. No, I think it was a "merry widow," maybe. A corset. But nobody ever burned anything.

Your story makes me wonder how many men actually hugged trees. When you were trashing these artifacts that you viewed as representing the oppression of women, were you seeing men, specifically men, as being the oppressors?

I don't think so, not in the early days. God knows, in the last twenty-five years, man as "the enemy" has certainly emerged; the separatist wing of the feminist movement is definitely present, no question about that. But in the early days, I think sexism was considered more a general societal problem.

You were the president of NOW during much of the effort to have the ERA ratified.

Right. But Ellie Smeal, who was the president of NOW after I was, devoted much of her effort to ratification.

Do you think it is fair to say that men opposed the ERA, that it was male chauvinism that was responsible for the failure of the ERA?

I would prefer to say that it was some male-dominated state legislatures that didn't vote yes on the ERA. We got thirty-five states. We needed thirty-eight. There were tiny numbers of women in those legislatures, but they were overwhelmingly voting yes on the ERA.

Do you think that those male legislators were listening to a certain woman from Illinois?

You mean Phyllis Schlafly?

Yes.

I think it's wrong to believe that men defeated the Equal Rights Amendment. I'm not a great believer in public opinion polls, and I think they were wrong in saying the majority of people supported the ERA. But even so, all the polls that I ever saw showed that more men supported ERA than women, which you might say is curious if you didn't understand what the issues were all about.

PHYLLIS SCHLAFLY
interviewed by Jack Kammer on *In a Man's Shoes*
WCVT (now WTMD) radio, Towson, Maryland
January 5, 1989

I think Phyllis Schlafly managed to play into people's fears. She talked about unisex bathrooms; she talked about homosexual marriage. She spoke of women in combat. Now we will have women in combat, but no ERA! It's very hard for me to use the phrase "male chauvinist," but I think if we had a fifty-fifty ratio of men and women in the state legislatures, I think we would have had the Equal Rights Amendment ratified, no question about it.

Of course, that's almost by definition. The women who get into state legislatures have to be sort of nontraditional women, whereas the men who are in state legislatures have to almost by definition be traditional men.

That certainly was true. It probably to some extent is true right now, but certainly was in the 1970s when we were doing this. Yes, that's a good point.

You have said that men have a lot of things in their lives that could stand some improvement.

Oh, absolutely. I don't know if this is your question, but the thing that interests me, if one does the laundry list of areas of men's lives that not only are different than women's but where they clearly seem to get the short end of the stick, it's my experience that most men don't see it as a problem. Let me give you a couple of specifics.

I do a lot of college speaking and I often raise the issue of compulsory draft registration. It would seem to me that men should be protesting draft registration. "My country can take me off and kill me" is what filling out that form indicates. Every time I mention that on a college campus, there will be maybe one or two guys who will say that they had considered this unfair, or that they hadn't thought about it, but after I mentioned it, they considered it unfair. But there certainly is not much response to that.

Another issue—less hypothetical, since we don't have an actual draft right now—is in dating. At the college level, of course, most of the people are dating. I talk about how unfair it is that usually the financial responsibility for dates is on guys. Many women are going to law school, or medical school, or plan to be architects or engineers, but somehow if they go out to dinner, it's still for the most part assumed the male is going to pick up the bill. Women may object to this on grounds that maybe it prevents impecunious but utterly delightful young men from seeing them socially, or because of the old idea that if somebody took you out to dinner, you were then expected to "put out" sexually. But mainly, if you go out to dinner, it's nice if somebody else pays the bill, right? I would think men would object simply on the grounds that it's unfair; why should they have to pay the bill? Lots of excuses are given. Men make more money, for instance. But college students don't make very much money whether they're male or female, and when people of the same gender go out socially, rarely do they prorate the bill to their IRS returns. But most men don't respond when I mention this.

What do you think might be getting in the way of men taking action on these issues? What needs to be done to get men to say, "You're right; this is wrong"?

Well, you mentioned the hugging and the drums, which a lot of people think is silly, but the general idea behind the hugging and the drums is a very valid one. In other words, men should start thinking about their role. And Bly's book, *Iron John,* was on the best-seller list for a long time, right? That meant somebody's reading it, and thinking men's roles have to be changed. Certainly many women don't want to change men's roles, but mainly I think it's men who don't want to change men's roles or they would make more effort to do so.

So what do you think is preventing men from doing something that would directly benefit them?

Well, this is a speculation and may be incorrect, but men with a lot of power in our society—who are a teensy fraction of the men—might not want to rock the boat, because things aren't going so badly for them. In other words, if I'm a powerful man and I'm making a fortune, and I don't have any responsibilities at home, and I don't care how much we pay for help, and I want my wife to take care of all the details of my life, and I have my secretary and my assistants, maybe I don't want a change; I like the way it is. But the vast majority of men, especially in the recession, are not in such comfortable shape—nervous wrecks, about losing jobs and so on. But maybe those men don't have a lot of power to change things. I don't know. There is also rampant homophobia among men: fear of being thought to be a sissy.

All the women who changed things didn't have a lot of power to change things. They got together and developed the power to change things.

It was mostly because of the numbers. At the beginning there were very few of us so-called leaders of the feminist movement. But we definitely struck a chord. Most women agreed, and agree, with us.

As you suggested, there are millions of men who are not very powerful. And even men who are making big bucks aren't necessarily happy. I get the idea that a lot of them feel aloof, alienated, distanced from their families, from their friends. They're very locked into narrow channels.

[Of 1,349 male senior-level executives interviewed] 68 percent are happy in their professional lives, but feel their family life suffers as a result. Of this group, nearly half admitted they regretted spending so many hours at the job and if they were to do it over, they would spend more time with their wife and children from the onset. Many brushed aside my questions with varying rationalizations, such as: You can't look back, You only have one chance to live life, or, I did what I had to do.

JAN HALPER, Ph.D.
Quiet Desperation: The Truth About Successful Men

Often they don't have "friend" friends. They have golfing buddies, but not friend friends.

So even those guys would have some reason to say, "Hey, you know, money ain't all that life is about."

It's a good question. I don't know what's keeping most men from exploring their gender issues. Happily, I think, more men are thinking about the male role, about how restrictive it is. I do know it's hard to have a sex-role revolution when only one sex is participating.

Barbara Dority

BARBARA DORITY is cofounder and cochair of the Northwest
Feminist Anti-Censorship Taskforce (NW-FACT) and executive
director of the Washington Coalition Against Censorship. She was
born in 1949.

Jack: *What's a feminist like you doing in a book like this?*

Barbara: The main purpose of NW-FACT is to provide a feminist voice, other than the one most people hear, on the issue of
whether all sexually explicit materials are intrinsically degrading
and harmful to women, so we are confronted with incredible prejudices against men.

How much of a feminist are you?

I am totally and completely a feminist. I worked for the passage
of the ERA for over four years. But recently it's been a real temp-
tation to stop using the word to describe myself, because meanings
have been attached to it by people with whom I do not agree, so
many people close their minds once they hear the word. But I'm
mighty stubborn about this, as are the others in NW-FACT. *We are
feminists* and we won't permit others to commandeer the term. The
dictionary says a feminist is a person who advocates or demands for
women the same rights granted to men. We add "rights *and responsibilities,*" because this is a big problem many women are having
today in the so-called feminist movement. They want the same
rights, but they don't want the same responsibilities.

Give me an idea of the responsibilities that you see some women not so interested in taking.

Many women are not interested in assuming responsibility for their part in the gender conflicts in our culture. Many women say they want to be equal to men, but they really don't. In fact, they want special protections. We often see this clearly in their proposed legislation. These protectionist tactics won't work—they are very self-destructive to women.

On the topic of protectionist tactics, what do you think of the Violence Against Women Act?

The [Violence Against Women] act, a 96-page bill first introduced last year and given a unanimous voice vote of approval by the Senate Judiciary Committee in October, proposes to "combat violence and crimes against women in the streets and in homes" with a wide array of weapons.

RORIE SHERMAN
National Law Journal
May 30, 1991

I'm appalled. I see no reason why violence against women is any more reprehensible than violence against men or why it should be punished more severely under the law. We're never going to get equality with this approach. There are responsibilities and risks involved with freedom.

Rate of Violent Crime 1979–1987, per 1,000 population
total: female victims: 24.7; male victims: 43.3
perpetrated by strangers: female victims: 11.4; male victims: 29.4

"FEMALE VICTIMS OF VIOLENT CRIME"
U.S. Department of Justice, Office of Justice Programs, Bureau of Justice Statistics
January 1991
victims age 12 and older

Do you have any idea what is motivating Senator Biden with his Violence Against Women Act?

I'm somewhat puzzled. Maybe he's trying to make up for the Anita Hill hearings, when his public stature in the eyes of many women declined drastically. I suspect he's doing a little pandering.

But he first proposed that law in 1990, before the Anita Hill hearings.

Yes, but he wasn't pursuing it then like he is now. He's much more adamant now, and determined to get it passed. But I don't think it will stand up to constitutional scrutiny.

> *Senator Joseph Biden, Chairman of the Senate Judiciary Committee:* In my house, being raised with a sister and three brothers, there was an absolute—a nuclear—sanction if under any circumstances, for any reason, no matter how justified—even self-defense—if you ever touched our sister, literally, not figuratively, literally. My sister, who's my best friend, my campaign manager, my confidante, grew up with absolute impunity in our household.
> *Sarah Buel, Founder of the Harvard Law School Battered Women's Advocacy Project:* She was a blessed woman.
> *Biden:* Uh huh, and I have the bruises to prove it. And I mean that sincerely. I'm not exaggerating when I say that.
>
> DURING SENATE JUDICIARY
> COMMITTEE HEARINGS
> on the Violence Against Women Act
> December 11, 1990
> as transcribed from videotape by the author

In speaking about women's responsibilities, do you have any thoughts about military obligations?

I've always felt that women should be equally subject to the draft—when it's necessary for the draft to be instituted. Of course, I have a problem with the whole current concept of the military. I came of age during the sixties, when so many young men were being shipped to Vietnam as cannon fodder. Even then, I was puzzled about why only men were forced to do this.

What do you think of the people who say, "Well, it's men who start the wars"?

I think that's a real cop-out. I can't accept the simplistic idea that "men rule the world." Some women support and contribute to wars just as some men do. But the vast majority of ordinary women *and* men are pawns and victims of war.

Why do you not agree with the idea that men rule the world?

Because women have equal, if not somewhat greater types of power than men do; it's simply in different areas where women are very powerful. In our society, rigid gender roles still dictate to mothers that they be the primary parent. Raising babies is a very powerful role. I'm not saying that we don't still have work to do on basic fairness and equality issues, but I am saying it's a mistake to make the blanket statement that the entire world is a patriarchy and that women have no power.

> In the form of absolute control over the body and soul of her child an immense kingdom was granted her.
>
> ALICE MILLER
> writing about her mother
> *Pictures of a Childhood: Sixty-six Watercolors and an Essay*

What other kinds of power do women have, beside raising babies?

In most developed countries, women are in charge of intimate relationships. I don't mean just sex, although certainly that is an important part. Women are in charge of intimate relationships, period. Men are taught that they don't know anything about relationships and that they must rely on women. Also, in Western culture, women have incredible power when a marriage breaks up.

How have you seen that power misused?

The system encourages divorcing women to be vindictive. Seattle is a relatively enlightened area, so I shudder to think how bad it is in other parts of the country. Here, the basic assumption of the family court is that the man is a jerk; he's deserting his wife—never mind if she left him; that doesn't make any difference—he's trying to walk away from his responsibilities, including his children. And that's the way he's treated. It's a very sad situation.

Generally, you're talking about male judges, are you not?

Actually, in a recent case I know quite well, the most abusive family court judge was a woman who is notorious for her vindictiveness and bias against men.

This might be an interesting place to talk about the strange relationship between conservatism and feminism. I am not sure it applies here, but would it be accurate to say that most of the female judges you are talking about are women who subscribe to the tenets of the women's movement and would call themselves feminists?

They probably would call themselves feminists, yes.

And would it be fair to say that most of the male judges, probably in their forties, fifties, and sixties, are a tad conservative and traditional?

Yes. Another example of the alliance between some feminists and conservatives. I never thought about that in the case of judges.

And they share the idea that men are jerks.

> You have never seen a bigger pain in the ass than the [divorced] father who wants to get involved; he can be repulsive. He wants to meet the kid after school at three o'clock, take the kid out to dinner during the week, have the kid on his own birthday, talk to the kid on the phone every evening, go to every open school night, take the kid away for a whole weekend so they can be alone together. This type of involved father is pathological.
>
> EX-JUDGE RICHARD HUTTNER
> quoted by Jane Young in
> New York magazine
> November 18, 1985

Yes. And the courts will go after a man for child support and throw him in jail if necessary, but they will not enforce his visitation rights with his own children. We *must* reform the law and give it some teeth to curb these abuses that some women commit. But we need a fundamental attitude change here, and I'm not sure how we can go about that.

What is the attitude currently?

That almost all men are jerks and *all* divorcing men are jerks and that men don't care about their children.

What's the attitude that women who think that way have about themselves?

They believe they're morally superior to men. They believe they are vastly better at parenting, because society has taught them that they are.

I have intimate knowledge of what it does to a man to be stripped of dignity, of control of any sort, to be looked upon as an intrinsically bad person. Sometimes, fathers just fall apart. Sometimes, in total despair and hopelessness, they leave the state, or even leave the country—because they *do* love their children and can't stand them being used as pawns. I detest the term *deadbeat dads*. All fathers who do this are not deadbeat dads. I ask women, "How would *you* feel if well over half your salary were forcibly taken from you with no accountability for its use, your ex-husband had total control of your children and wouldn't honor your visitation rights and the courts wouldn't either, and the father of your children was filling their heads with vindictive lies about you? How long could you deal with that sort of abuse and heartbreak?"

Contrary to popular belief, a divorced father who disappears from his children's lives is not necessarily an irresponsible, uncaring man who jettisons his family for unburdened freedom and a swinging life. While this stereotype is justified in some instances, the reasons are more complex in others, some researchers and counselors say. Sometimes, a father drops out of his children's lives because, paradoxically, he cares too much, rather than too little.

JOAN SWEENEY
Los Angeles Times
December 23, 1982

Well said. I want to switch gears here and ask a rhetorical question. From time to time I contribute brief items on gender issues to the Mantrack section of Playboy. Should I be ashamed?

Of course not. I find absolutely nothing offensive about *Playboy* magazine.

What do you think of the idea that it degrades women?

I think it's ridiculous. One would have to believe that the human body is intrinsically dirty and degrading to believe that a magazine that contains pictures of nude women is automatically degrading to women. This sort of Victorian prudery is leading the women's movement in the wrong direction.

What do the data show about a connection between sexually explicit material and crimes against women?

Evidence for a causal connection is nonexistent. Even the notorious Meese Commission, formally known as the Attorney General's Commission on Pornography, under the Reagan administration had to conclude that there was no real evidence of such a connection. But antipornography feminists and religious conservatives continue to spread the lie that the commission concluded the opposite, so many people believe it did.

> To seize upon the "men's magazines" as the causal factor [in rape] would be unjustified, as the [Meese] Commission apparently recognized when it conceded:
>> While these results offer correlational evidence, again, they do not support any causal link between readership of such [men's] magazines and sexually aggressive behavior. (p. 951)
>
> The Commission concluded that "at most" it could say only that the relationship between rape rates and circulation rates of adult magazines is "plausible" (p. 952).
>
> Shirley Feldman-Summers, Ph.D.
> "A Comment on the Meese Commission Report and the Dangers of Censorship"
> *Sexual Coercion and Assault*, Volume 1 (6), 1986

Thinking of the Meese Commission, does the right wing feel more strongly about violence against women than it feels about violence against men?

I'm sure they do. In their ideology, women are weak and helpless creatures that are owned and protected by men.

And many feminists are looking at the other side of the same wall: men are crude and women need protection from them.

Sure. They're saying that women are morally superior to men and it's women's job to control men.

What do you think of the possibility that what really outrages many feminists about erotica isn't that it degrades women, but that it's enjoyable to men?

I think that's a part of it. But perhaps more importantly, they are often terrified of their own sexuality. I think most women still view sex as something they trade for marriage, financial security, and fidelity. So the idea that women can enjoy sex for its own sake without these things is very frightening to them.

What do you think of the idea that women are not as interested as men in sexually explicit images?

Research does indicate that men are more visually sexually stimulated than women.

Do you think there are any types of erotica that are more appealing to women that we could make an equally ridiculous argument to try to ban?

Well, there are those amazing "bodice rippers."

The romance novels?

"Bodice rippers," I call them. The covers always show an extremely powerful man overpowering a woman as she swoons into his arms. The woman doesn't like him at first because he's a strong, dark, silent rogue, but as the story progresses and he continues to pursue her, eventually she thinks, "Wow, I guess he really does turn me on," which he has from the beginning, of course. Then some horrible incident occurs and he saves her and carries her off to live happily ever after. This is the classic Victorian patriarchal image.

But we don't see feminists out there trying to make laws to ban romance novels. In bodice rippers, men are power and security objects—which men are in our culture anyway—and women respond to that sexually. Some feminists believe women are only sexual objects. I really don't see the difference.

Earlier you said that women control relationships. Could we broaden that statement to say that women control morality, that women are the arbiters of what's moral and what's immoral?

Yes, I think we could say that.

And what we're seeing is that what women enjoy is not ruled immoral, but what men enjoy is?

Yes. Another part of the problem that women have with sexually explicit material is that men enjoy looking at women they don't know. The idea that this reduces the value of an individual woman's sexual "product" humiliates me. A lot of things that many so-called feminists say and do humiliate me.

In a speech you gave in Canada, you talked about what happens to a woman who dares to speak up against the standard feminist line of thinking. What does happen?

Well, male-bashers such as Andrea Dworkin and Catharine MacKinnon have said that FACT groups are "the Uncle Toms of the women's movement." We've been called child pornographers. We've been called women-haters, because we oppose censorship of sexually explicit materials.

A little later on in your speech, you said, "I shall leave it to your imagination what happens to the few brave (or naive) men who commit the ultimate sacrilege of questioning and objecting to the vicious feminist characterizations of themselves as a class of malignant, violent rapists and misogynists." You can leave it to my imagination because I have an idea of what it's like, but for those people who are reading this book, whose imaginations might not have so much raw material to work with, how would you describe what happens to such men?

They are cut off from women and get a bad reputation. The word spreads quickly that they're misogynists, that they're "in denial," that they refuse to admit their problem and work on it. They're viciously attacked; they become social outcasts.

What do you think less-militant women might do to let it be known that the militants who have captured the media are misrepresenting how women feel about men?

The only answer I have is the long arduous process of education. Speak up with your women friends when you hear these incredible assumptions that are made about men. There are lots of women who don't fall for the man-hating line, who are having relationships with men whom they love and respect, yet they still engage in male-bashing because it's the socially acceptable thing to do. So I suggest to women that the next time they find themselves in one of those conversations, stop and say, "Have you ever thought about these things we say about our men? Do you actually believe this is really true?" I've seen things change immediately in a group of women when somebody does that, because many of them *don't* really believe it, they just think they *should* believe it. All I can suggest is just don't go along with it. Speak up. Don't just sit passively by. "Silence is the voice of complicity."

Women must realize that it's not in their best interest, or in the best interest of their intimate relationships with men, to maintain these ridiculous stereotypes. I often think men eventually give up and figure, "Well, if that's how she thinks I am, I may as well be that way. If that's what she thinks, then why should I be any more responsible, or any more loyal, or any more anything? She's never going to give me credit for it anyway."

People tend to live up to expectations.

Or down to them. They certainly do.

Char Tosi

CHAR TOSI is the founder, president and owner of Woman Within, Inc., an organization seeking to initiate women in reclaiming the strength, power and wisdom of the light and dark sides of the deep feminine. She is a registered nurse with a master's degree in counseling and was a professor of nursing for fifteen years at the University of Wisconsin–Milwaukee. Her husband, Rich Tosi, is president of the New Warrior Network, an organization whose goal is to initiate men in identifying and focusing on their life's mission. Together, Char and Rich conduct couples weekends for women and men who have been through Woman Within and New Warrior. She and Rich live in Fenton, Michigan and have two grown sons. Char was born in 1944.

Jack: *Before Rich became involved in the New Warriors and before you started Woman Within, what was your relationship like?*

Char: We were both asleep. We were very unconscious. We were going through our life as our mothers and fathers instructed us. I used to iron all my husband's shirts. When we first dated I even ironed his underwear, which is what my mother did. I laugh about it now, but it was my way to please, to get acceptance, to make sure he would stay with me and depend on me and wouldn't leave me. Then he started working with men to develop the New Warriors. I felt abandoned, which is one of my central issues. He spent all kinds of time with the men, and before, we spent all our time together, even though it wasn't healthy time. He was the only married man of the three cofounders of the New Warrior Network. They were dating and I could see the excitement in them, and their life-style really threatened me. Rich and I had been married fifteen years and I was afraid of losing Rich to this other path of singlehood and romance. Then there came a time when he did not "need me" anymore the way he used to need me, and we separated for eight months. In retrospect I really do support our time apart; he needed time away from me to get in touch with who he was as a man, and I needed to discover myself apart from him. My abandonment issues and my insecurity issues pushed me to a new place of growth.

When Rich left, was there any assurance that he was coming back?

No, except for my intuition. There was a piece of me that felt the connection between us very deeply, and I had faith. Actually, I went through the stage of asking "Do I really want this man? Do I still want to be with him?" I had to make a decision, too.

Your handling of this was an indication of some pretty deep strength and health on your part. There might be other women who would have not handled it so well. Can you describe how other women might have handled it that would not have led to the happy consequence that yours has led to?

Yes. I've seen many women who have gotten violent. They have carried it out by damaging their partner's car, doing other damaging things to act out the abandonment in a revengeful way, similar to what is portrayed in the movie *War of the Roses.*

What does that lead to?

It just leads to a cycle of hatred, more conflict, deeper pain and wounds in the relationship.

And it only enhances the man's need for feeling like he needs separation?

Sure. And he needs to continue to protect himself even more deeply.

Does this tell us anything about why there might be—or why there has been in popular culture, in the media—a lot of ridiculing of men's work,

*the men's movement, New Warriors, Robert Bly and all of those things?
Does it suggest why we're making fun of that?*

Yes. I think women are really threatened to have men come into
their own strength and power. Because women are threatened, they
become—I'm going to use a particular word right now—a bitch. I
think women have tremendous power with their tongue and with
their bitchy side to castrate men. I have seen and felt that from
women. I have talked at men's conferences and I have heard from
men's hearts that they are frightened to death of that part of the
feminine power.

Why didn't you use your power that way?

I probably did in some ways. I have gotten to the place where it's
important that my husband sees my bitch and still stays present
for me.

Because the shadow is always there along with the good stuff?

That's right. If the wild bitch can't come out and feel safe with
him, she's going to get him somewhere else.

She'll turn into a monster?

That's right. And we've had to do a lot of work around that. I
want to define what I mean by a woman's bitch. The bitch is there
to protect the little girl—the little girl inside the woman—which in
my case was the part of me that feared being abandoned by my
husband. When the little girl feels threatened and hurt, the bitch
comes out to protect her just like the bitch dog protects her pup-
pies. What happens a lot of times is the bitch part of women brings
out the fearful little boy in men, so they have to protect back. It
becomes a dance; actually it becomes a war.

*What's the male counterpart of the bitch? What's protecting the little
boy in the man?*

It's interesting. We had that discussion once at a men's conference and we didn't really come up with a particular word.

Prick, bastard?

Perhaps.

Jerk, asshole, something like that? Heartless brute? It's more diffuse, isn't it?

Right, it is. There wasn't anything quite as poignant.

What does the bitch want for the little girl?

She wants her to never be hurt again.

So the bitch is motivated by love?

Right, exactly. Love for herself. If the woman is conscious that she's using her bitch to protect the little girl, it's a lot safer for her and also for the man she's dealing with. A lot of women operate out of the bitch and they don't understand where the bitch is coming from.

And what does that lead to?

It just leads to more destruction. It leads to more distance in the relationship. It's unconscious; women don't even know what they're doing. It's that anger that comes from a real deep place, the anger that cuts so fiercely. In fact, as much as men are afraid of that part of women, women are afraid of it in themselves and in each other.

Because it doesn't match their view of the kind of person they're supposed to be?

I think it goes into what I consider fear of the feminine.

Women's own fear of the feminine?

The dark feminine.

Tell me.

The dark feminine is the part that destroys. The light feminine is that part that creates, that gives life, that bears children—which is something that men can't do, can't experience in the way of carrying a child in their own body. The dark feminine balances the creative force. Women can give life; women can also destroy very deeply. That's where I think that negative energy plays itself out. If it's not owned, it just gets bigger and bigger and bigger, and I think women project it onto men. They see the killer part of men and let men carry their dark feminine. They see it in rapists. They see it in war, especially the pacifists, and what's missing is that they can't see it in themselves.

We do an exercise with our leaders where we instruct them to tap into their wild, destructive energy and then they express it through movement and voice and facial expressions. It is phenomenal how it frees up their creative energy. As long as that destructive energy is blocked, the creative is blocked as well. It's directly proportional. This experience also allows women to own their destructive energy and feel its power. This can be very frightening for women to see in other women as well as in themselves. It's also frightening for men. In my relationship with my husband, I want to get permission from him before I let my bitch out in his presence.

So he can be assured that it will be under control?

Right, and that I'll know he'll stay present for that part of me. I've let it out without warning and it's caused an incredible wound in him. What I want to do as a woman is not to wound him. I want him to see that part of me and still love me, but I don't want to use it as a sword to kill him.

You want him to love the whole woman?

Yes. Right.

Okay. Let me go back for a second. In what regard do you hold the part that men play in creating life?

Men create the external environment by providing and protecting. This is like creating a womb for women, so they can be safe to create internally. My husband has made it safe for me to create from my womb, not only my children, but also my career. He has been willing to provide the primary income while I follow my bliss. There may come a time when we switch roles, but the deep, primal nature of man is to create ways to provide and protect. When women interfere with this, they are taking away an essential part of men's souls and their own souls.

And so you see the creation of life as being exclusively a feminine function?

In this context that we're talking about right now it feels like the feminine function.

Let's talk a bit about that. Do you know the idea of male pregnancy?

No.

Before I explain it I want to preface by saying I do not mean this at all to demean or to denigrate the magic of women's part in the creation of life.

Okay. I honor that.

What I want to do is to elevate men's part in the creation of life, because men need to be much more balanced between their creative and their destructive forces.

Sure.

I was raised to think that the uterus, the womb, was a sort of magical vessel. It was a magic I sadly felt no part of. And then I read an article in Omni magazine* about male pregnancy. Some scientists were doing ovarian-cancer research and they wanted to study how the absence of female hormones would affect fetal development, so they implanted a baboon zygote, a fertilized egg, in a male baboon's abdomen. The zygote sent out a placenta, found a supply of blood, developed its sac and started growing. So the magic in the creation of life is in the zygote, the union of male and female, not the uterus. It's the zygote that reaches out and says "I want to live, I want to live, I want to live." And when I read that I thought, "I like that a lot!" because it means that my male magic of creating life is on a par with the female magic of creating life.

That's true. I do believe that.

In our culture generally, do you think that the male contribution, the male connection to the creation of life, is recognized and honored?

No, I do not. I think women tend to—and I think men buy into this, too—put male sexuality in a context of being bad and destructive.

If my sperm is just a toxic waste, if it really has no magic to it, what do I care? I'll throw it around.

Yes.

* *Omni*, December 1985, page 50

If a man doesn't have an appreciation of his creative capacity, his life-giving capacity, and has an exaggerated focus on his destructive capacity, what can we see is likely to happen?

I think they don't focus on all the different aspects of themselves. Also, if society is projecting all that destructive energy onto men, then men act it out in ways that are harmful. My challenge for women is to withdraw those projections, to stop seeing destructiveness and competition in men only and start seeing it equally in themselves, so that men are relieved of carrying that entire burden alone, and can develop in a lot of other ways.

I think women see men as having power, and I don't think they understand what woman power is. I believe that women often function from a place of not being enough, not good enough, a place of insecurity and low self-esteem. They replace that insecurity with false power, with wanting to have power over men. One of the most effective ways I have seen women using to gain power over men is by shaming men, using their tongue to put men down, to shame their sexuality, to shame their success. Because of this, men have had to erect enormous walls, high walls, thick walls to protect themselves. In my experience of working with couples, I have seen the vulnerability of men and their willingness to let down their walls with women. What I have observed is the thicker and higher the wall, the more vulnerable is the man. It's so healing for couples to discover that.

So are you suggesting that the thick walls are erected precisely because what's inside is so tender?

That's exactly what I'm saying, and it's too risky for men to let women see that, because women aren't aware of how sharp their tongues are and how quickly they can destroy that part of the man.

So what does this tell us about "sensitive men," men who pretend to have no walls? I once wrote a piece that said men are too sensitive to be more sensitive, that calluses build up over sensitive skin to defend against repeated irritation, and to tell a man to be more sensitive without doing anything to remove the irritation is actually asking him to be more insensitive.

That's exactly what I'm saying. I believe men first of all need to feel safe and accepted by other men before they can open up to a woman.

Is that because men are less likely to shame other men, at least in a group, where shaming is against the rules?

Right, exactly. And I think that at least in the generation of men today, who were raised mainly by women, many mothers did shame them and squelch their magic, and I think that pattern continues in many marriage relationships, where the woman can have a lot of power in shaming, and keeping the man in place.

What are the handles on his psyche that she uses to hold him in place? What are the targets for shame that she'll shoot at?

Not providing enough money is one big one. His sexuality is another, either wanting too much sex or too little sex, or being too rough. It goes in all different directions around sexuality. I think money and sex are the two big places that women shame men.

The brochure for Woman Within uses a phrase that's pretty interesting: "the angry, rebellious adolescent." Do you see many women today acting as angry, rebellious adolescents?

Actually, I think many feminists are acting like angry, rebellious adolescents. They are trying to decide who they are and what they want out of life, and acting out their anger. Anger allows the adolescent to separate from the parents and go forward. I think a lot of women are emotionally stuck in the stage of adolescence.

What would you say to women who are looking to move out of that stage?

I would say they need to tap into the real source of their anger. In our workshops we help them access that anger and release it in a healthy way. A lot of women are terrified of their own anger, and they deny its existence. It comes out not in a raised voice necessarily, but it's the quick tongue. I think the gift of women is being able to articulate, sometimes in a hurtful way.

I've also heard some really, really angry women who at the right moment—on radio and TV, for instance—can sound sweet and mellifluous as they vent their venom.

That's right. To my mind those are very dangerous women. They scare me because they have not touched that part of themselves.

Can we say who, which parent, most feminists think they're angry at?

I think it's the patriarchy, men. If the patriarchy would just change or if men would change, then everything would be fine and then women would get everything they want.

What do you think of this idea of patriarchy?

I think patriarchy has created wounds in men as well as women. I see it as a concept that's changing and I'm really encouraged by that. I'm not so sure that matriarchy is the answer at all.

Women will blame the patriarchy because it's easier to look at men's faults than women's faults.

Right. That's the projection of shadow we were talking about.

Do you think it's scary for women to think that maybe an appropriate target for their anger is not the other, but themselves? Not the other group, but their own culture, the female culture?

Definitely. That's what we're working on—being angry at those women who were not there to initiate us, and who were not there to honor us as women. A lot of women's anger has gone underground, and operates from a subtle place of control and power through manipulation. I feel that women have tended to take on a lot of control that they don't really realize they have, just as an acting-out adolescent has a tremendous amount of control in a family. The attention is focused on them, they get feedback—maybe negative feedback, but they get feedback, or strokes, whatever you want to call it—and they can thrive on that.

If America is a family and the government is the patriarchy and feminism is our troubled adolescent daughter, are the media the mother who gives her all the attention she demands?

That's an interesting metaphor. I never put it that way.

What does the New Warrior training do for men?

From my perspective, it empowers men to own parts of themselves that they cut off, which is, I'm sure, different for every man, but often it's the ability to speak out, the ability to face themselves, other men and women, and tell them that they—the men—are okay.

It develops the ability of men to say, "Hey, if we have a problem, it's not just me"?

Exactly. Also, it provides them a different group of men, rather than just playing football or going to a bar and drinking. It provides that at an emotional level.

Let's talk for a minute about those guys at the bar. A lot of guys are not going to New Warrior, it's just too much for them right now. It might be too much for them forever; they'll never go.

That's right.

What's the littlest, teeniest, tiniest little piece that a man might say to his buddy while they're drinking at a bar that might begin the process of becoming the strong men they need to be?

The teeniest, tiniest piece? As I see the wounds that are really healed through the Warriors, the father relationship is a big one. Maybe it would be to encourage a guy to talk about his father.

So just saying, "Hey, tell me about your old man. What was your old man like?" might be an interesting conversation starter.

Right.

That's pretty nonthreatening.

Right. I think movies have been reflecting that wound. *Field of Dreams* comes to mind, and there are others that have a lot of father-son unresolved wounds. Yeah, even the movies are beginning to tap into that consciousness. That's a good sign.

Jane Chastain

JANE CHASTAIN was the nation's first female sportscaster, on both the local and the national levels, and spent seventeen years covering sports. She is now a political commentator for Crawford Broadcasting, a chain of radio stations throughout America, a regular panelist on the cable television show "CNN & Company," and the author of *I'd Speak Out on the Issues If I Only Knew What to Say*. Jane is married, has a teenage son and lives in Los Angeles.

Jack: *I first got the idea to invite you to participate in this book when I saw you on the Faith Daniels show. You effectively and good-naturedly countered a woman who was advocating that women should go on strike for a day to protest employment discrimination. You have done great things not just to protest, but to overcome employment discrimination against women. How do you see your style differing from the style of the woman advocating the strike?*

Jane: Her proposal for a strike seemed like a classic case of bellyaching and complaining, quite frankly. It reminded me of something I heard as a child on the playground. "Nobody likes me, everybody hates me, think I'll go eat worms." That kind of attitude didn't work when I was a child on the playground, and I don't think it works in society today.

What kind of children on the playground would intone that little ditty?

Well, I think all of us go through periods of self-pity, but I think that it's more than that today. There is a saying that applies here: "You're never a failure until you blame somebody else."

As you were beginning your career, you had an incident you told me about earlier that could have given you a very good excuse to just throw up your hands and say, "Oh, poor me; I'll never make it in this business."

Yes. I was still quite young, I had worked very hard for several years to try to break into television. I had been going to lots of auditions, taking lots of classes, doing a lot of television commercials, modeling and that sort of thing, but finally I got my big break making football predictions on a television station in Atlanta, the CBS affiliate there. The sports director came on to me and professed his love for me out of the blue one day. And, yes, I was young and vulnerable, but not that vulnerable. So I said, "Thanks, but no thanks." He did his best after that to make my work life miserable. If that had been the only job I ever had, I would have viewed all women as victims and all men as brutes. I endured, didn't tolerate, but endured for a short while the subtle backstabbing and sabotage that followed. You have this kind of friction on the job against men, too, especially in a field as competitive as TV, so it's hard to know how much of the difficulty was a result of rebuffing this man's advances. But I shudder to think about the number of women who stay in those oppressive situations. I left shortly thereafter and took a job in Raleigh, North Carolina.

One of the best times of my life was when I was covering the Miami Dolphins the year they were the only perfect team in National Football League history. It was 1972, and they went 17 and 0, all the way to winning the Super Bowl. I never once saw the quarterback run off the field to Coach Shula and say, "That mean old linebacker won't let me get to where I want to go." I mean, you'd be out of there! And in your career, you don't complain. You do what you have to do to get to your goal.

My boss at WTVJ in Miami, Bernie Rosen, taught me what it meant to be a good sportscaster. When he sent you out to do a story, you'd better get the story! He was tough, but he was very, very fair. I remember when I first came to Miami, George Wilson was the coach of the Dolphins. And he apparently was kidding my boss about hiring a woman, and he said something like, "Well, she won't come to my camp," and Bernie said, "Oh, yes, she will!" He just wasn't going to take this lying down. Wilson later claimed he was kidding initially, but Bernie didn't take it that way. So Wilson backed down a bit and said, "Well, she won't interview me!" My first day on the job in Miami was opening day of the Dolphins training camp, and guess where Bernie sent me. The Dolphins training camp, of course. I did my stories that day, and everything was fine, but I heard a rumor that Coach Wilson wouldn't give me an interview. I questioned Bernie about it, and he said yes, that was true. So the next time I was at camp, I went up to Coach Wilson and I explained to him that I had heard this, and that this was a real problem for my station, and was there anything that I had done, or was there anything I could do, to correct this? And he explained to me—he was kind of embarrassed—that it was a joke that had gotten out of hand and he just couldn't back down; he didn't want to lose face.

I said, "It may be a thing between you and Bernie, but it's embarrassing to me. It makes me look bad." And he said, "I promise, if anybody asks me why, I'll tell them." That night, on the Larry King radio show, which was down in Miami at that time, someone called in and said, "I think it's great that you won't give that woman an interview, because women belong in the kitchen." And Wilson explained the whole thing just as he said he would. But after I spoke with him, I made many, many trips to the Dolphins camp, and Coach Wilson always treated me like a nonentity, like I was not there. I don't know if it was because he was embarrassed or because he thought I might ask him again, and I might pressure him. But later on in the season, I noticed that he would at least acknowledge my presence, just with a nod or something. And near the end of the season he said to me, "Jane, are you going to be here tomorrow?" And I said, "Yes." And he said, "Well, I'll give you that interview." I had just written it off because I was so sure he was absolutely not going to back down to Bernie. But after the interview, the players—who had also been very, very aware of what was going on, although they never really spoke about it—they ran over and picked me up and threw me in the Dumpster. And it was like saying, "Okay, you've made it; you've been accepted; you're one of us. Congratulations."

Now, why is it that you perceived being thrown into a Dumpster to be a friendly gesture, rather than harassment or hostility?

Well, I think it *was* a friendly gesture. I hadn't tried to make an issue of what Wilson was doing. I never went up to those players and bellyached and complained about their boss; I never put them in a compromising position of having to talk to me about what an awful person Coach Wilson was. I think the fact that I didn't make an issue out of it is actually what caused him to address it. If you have a disagreement with somebody and you try to back them up against the wall, then they get caught up in defending themselves rather than examining their own position to see if it's tenable.

What is your observation of what happened between Lisa Olson, the Boston Herald *sportswriter, and the New England Patriots football players?*

I'll tell you about that in just one second. I want to cover another incident with Al Davis, the owner of the Raiders football team. My boss sent me off to do an interview and Davis refused to let me interview him. He didn't want to be interviewed by a woman. So I just said, "Well, is there a reason?" No. He didn't really explain; he didn't want to explain. He just didn't want to do it. And so, again, I thought I wanted him to reexamine what he had done, rather than to make an issue out of it. And I said, "Well, fine. Tony,"—Tony Segretto, now the number one sportscaster in Miami, was my camera man—"Tony, set up the camera, show me what buttons to push, and show me how to move the camera. I'll give you the questions to ask Mr. Davis, and Mr. Davis, I'll let my cameraman do the interview with you." And Tony was showing me and I was giving him the questions, and we just went right ahead like it was no problem. And before I turned the camera on, Al Davis said, "No, no, that's all right. I changed my mind. You can do the interview."

What do you think there was about what you did that impressed him?

I don't know that I impressed him, but again by not making him an enemy, by not making it him-against-me, I think he had a chance to examine his stand and deal with his own conscience. The same thing happened with Joe DiMaggio, when he was in town. He had retired as a player, and was not in baseball at the time. He was staying at the Yankee Clipper, where he and Marilyn Monroe had honeymooned, and my boss sent me up to interview him. I was going to ask him some sports questions, and he, I think, thought that I was going to try to dig up something in his past that perhaps he didn't want to talk about. And so he didn't want to do the interview. He was very hostile in the beginning.

Did he think you were a life-style reporter rather than . . .

I don't know; we didn't even use the term "life-style" then. But I asked him the first couple of questions, and he was so stilted and cold. And then about the second or third question, he kind of relaxed and said, "Oh, you really do know what you're talking about, don't you?" And he just relaxed and gave me a great interview.

But about Lisa Olson and her allegation of being harassed by the New England Patriots, I have to say that I think a reporter's job is to basically be invisible, and to do the best job of bringing the subject out. I was never in favor of women going into men's locker rooms. And this is the reason why: I knew a lot of female athletes, and I pictured the corresponding fairness issue for them if women were allowed to go into male locker rooms. I just wouldn't do that to my women friends who were tennis players and other types of athletes. I didn't think they should have to give interviews in various stages of undress, and to me, fair was fair. Now, this is a wonderful example of how men really tend to defer to women almost to a fault, to the point where they don't press for fairness from women. You still will not find any men demanding access—not one who's taken seriously anyway—to the females' dressing rooms. They have not allowed male reporters in there. And yet on the other side, in the male locker room, everyone is afraid to say no.

The few times that I was in a locker room, I was covering basketball, the NBA Game of the Week, for the CBS network. I was doing after-game interviews and my producers insisted that they wanted the locker-room atmosphere. So I would go and talk to the coaches ahead of time, and I would tell them that I would have my camera set up so that I was facing the wall by the door, and to please tell the players that as soon as I did my interview I would leave.

And I always did that. I respected their privacy. Now that didn't mean I was a prude; I'd been married for a number of years and I didn't expect to see anything that I hadn't seen before, but on the other hand, I'm human, and they're human. I remember once I was doing an interview with one of the basketball players, and a big roar went up in the locker room, and I was just hoping that whoever it was didn't walk in front of the camera, because I just knew that someone was pulling something. And later I found out that a player had come in and flashed, but I was busy doing my interview. If it had been after the interview, I probably would have noticed.

He flashed you?

He was probably just trying to get a laugh out of the other players, and he knew I was busy and occupied; it was a very quick thing. But in all my years covering sports, I never missed a deadline, never failed to get a good interview because I couldn't go into the locker room. I always sent word that I was outside with a camera crew. I told them I needed an interview and who I wanted, and they always sent them right out.

The situation that I heard about with Lisa Olson was that she was hanging around in their locker room after a practice session. And I felt this was unnecessary. So I'm afraid I just didn't have a lot of sympathy for her, because my opinion was that she was trying to exploit the situation. And again, it absolutely amazes me, that the men have not demanded fairness. I think it shows that men have more respect for women than sometimes women do for men. And I think that's really a sad commentary. It makes me embarrassed for my sex, quite frankly.

> As the season began, [Lisa Olson's] relationship with the players appeared to be fine. One criticism was brought to the attention of the Patriots management prior to the events of September 17. Two players had complained to James Oldham, the Patriots' Director of Media Relations, and to Patrick Sullivan, the Patriots' General Manager, that they felt Olson was spending too much time in the locker room, standing around without interviewing anyone. They felt she was a "looker."
>
> . . . The Patriots management had made no effort to raise the

> problem with [other] players to determine whether or not others had the same perception (as some now report) and, if so, to discuss whether the perception was correct and what should be done. Potentially incendiary rumors were left to explode in the locker room on September 17.
>
> Report of Special Counsel Philip B. Heymann to the Commissioner of the National Football League Paul Tagliabue
> November 7, 1990

People talk about men not respecting women. Well, I worked almost exclusively with men during my whole seventeen years as a sportscaster. I have found men to have an exceptional sense of decency and fair play. I think of lot of that probably comes from athletics, where there's an emphasis on good sportsmanship.

Is your point of view on these issues widely held by women in the broadcast industry?

Not at all. Let me tell you about a discussion panel I was on, called Working with Men. It was during a workshop at the National Convention of American Women in Radio and Television. It began with a rap video on misogyny, and it went downhill from there. They talked about the Glass Ceiling and discrimination and sexual harassment and Anita Hill and stereotyping. As I sat there, I toyed with the idea of just saying things that would make everyone feel warm and fuzzy—you know, maybe I should just go with the flow. I toyed with that idea for only about two seconds, and then decided that the audience was young women who were trying to get ahead in broadcasting, and that the best thing I could do for them would be to tell them the truth about why some women don't make it to the top. I told them how my goals changed when I was in a hotel room in Mexico City, when I was covering the Pan-American Games for CBS back in 1975. When I called home every night and I heard my baby cry, that's when my own priorities changed. And it didn't take me long to discover that the quality of time I was able to give my family was actually in an inverse ratio to the quantity of time that I spent on my job. I talked about the fact that sixty-one percent of the nation's top female executives are childless compared to only fourteen percent of the women in the general population. And I talked about the fact that even when you compare the professions like medicine and law, you find, for instance, that female physicians take fewer patients per hour, and choose to work fewer hours, than do male physicians. It's hard to point to a Glass Ceiling in a female doctor's own office. So as long as women have a choice between staying home with their children and working full-time, I just don't think that we're going to see the same ratio of women to men in the executive suite as in the general work force. And I wasn't bringing this up to discourage them, but rather to encourage them. I wanted to be sure that they didn't see obstacles that weren't there, and that they didn't create obstacles for themselves. That they see the choices are their choices.

Perhaps men miss their kids, too?

Well, of course. I think they do.

Is it your belief that if a woman decides that she's going to focus on her career, in the same way that the man traditionally focuses on his career, that she has about an equal chance of getting to the top as the guy does?

I really believe, from my own experience, that it's probably even better than equal today. I think that if a woman has taken the right courses and preparation, if she enters a company through the right track—one of the line positions like engineering or sales, not a support function like personnel or public relations—if she creates the same kind of record that a man does, she has at least an equal shot.

A U.S. Census Bureau study shows . . . women in their early 20s now make slightly more than men their age. Pay is about equal for women and men in their late 20s and early 30s but the gap starts to widen for women who are 40 and older.

"Take a 45-year-old woman," [Harvard economist Claudia] Goldin said. "If she went to college she went at a time when she majored in English literature, but her male counterpart majored in engineer-

: ing. She's now probably in a career she never dreamed she'd be in
: and she didn't prepare in the same way a man did," she said. "Your
: 25-year-old has a much better idea of what she's going to be when
: she grows up."
:
:
: United Press International
: April 19, 1993

*Do you sometimes get the feeling that many of the complaints we hear
about unfairness to women are an attempt to get around the necessity of
working hard and making tough choices?*

Oh, I don't think there's any question about it. You don't get to
the top job on flextime.

*It makes me wonder how flextime and the Glass Ceiling can both be
feminist issues.*

Yes. You've got to decide what your priorities are. If you've got
a clearly defined goal, if you're focused on your career, and if you've
put in the proper training and the proper preparation, you can
succeed. That doesn't mean my priorities are right and yours are
wrong. And it doesn't mean that somebody's going to hand you the
job. Sometimes you've got to be like that quarterback in the football game. When there are no openings and nobody's willing to
move over and let you in, you've got to lateral. Sometimes you've
got to be willing, and men do it all the time, to change jobs.

Again, I think of the quarterback as he looks down the field.
He's trained to see the opening, not the obstacle.

Gayle Kimball

GAYLE KIMBALL, Ph.D., is the coordinator of women's studies at California State University, Chico. She is the author of three books, including *The 50-50 Marriage* and *50-50 Parenting*. She is completing a book entitled *Empowering Parents*, and is the editor of *Women's Culture* and *Everything You Need to Know to Succeed After College*. Gayle is in her forties and is the joint-custodial mother of a teenage son.

Jack: *Do you remember the fathers' rights conference you attended in Denver in 1987?*

Gayle: Yes. When you introduced me to the audience you said, "I'm going to use the F word."

I did?

Everybody thought, "What's he going to say?" Then you said, "She's a feminist," and they laughed.

As a feminist, did you feel welcome at that conference?

Yes, because I presented a workshop about shared custody. They knew that I was sympathetic with their goal of being involved fathers.

What was the feeling you detected in the men?

Pain. A lot of suffering and pain. And it's justified. I can't think of a worse feeling than having no control or access or shared time with your kids. My heart goes out to those guys when I talk with them. I feel their frustration, their longing and their loss.

A lot of people are not so sympathetic to men. What do you think of male-bashing?

It's unfair to blame men when we have socialized them to act like "Marlboro men." I think we have to step back and look at the messages we give boys and young men about being tough, for instance, if we complain that men aren't disclosive enough. It's imperative to understand that boys and girls are raised in different cultures. We shouldn't expect that the other gender has the same viewpoints as our own culture. For example, Deborah Tannen's books, *You Just Don't Understand* and *That's Not What I Meant*, explain how men's and women's languages are different, which can be frustrating if we're not aware.

American guys had better toughen up! Judging by the results of a new national *Redbook* survey of 500 women . . . male-bashing is on the rise. . . . The worst male-bashers? Women under the age of 25. Almost half of them have been accused of putting a man down for no reason. And two out of three say they have no plans to stop.

> sidebar to an article on male-bashing
> by Judy Markey
> *Redbook*
> May 1993

And if that point isn't understood, what's likely to result?

Blame. Criticism. "You're a jerk." But if I understand your socialization process, how your culture works, then I can be empathetic.

Young men get the message that they have to make a lot of money to care for their families. That seems to be a key problem in socialization.

I think young people in their twenties are discouraged about making a lot of money. They don't have the same kind of expectations as the earlier generation did—to graduate from college and do better than their parents. Studies show that people in their twenties expect that they're going to be in dual-earner households. There are not very many women out there who expect to find Prince Charming to take care of them. Each semester in my college classes I assign an essay. I simply ask, "Describe a typical weekday in your life fifteen years from now." My students expect that both the man and woman will be working, although often the man will be the main provider. The woman may work part-time or have flexible scheduling or take long maternity leave.

In your experience, are young women preparing themselves for careers as vigorously as young men are?

Absolutely. They know there's a fifty percent divorce rate in recent marriages, so they've gotten the message that they need to provide some kind of financial base for themselves and their future children.

When young men look into the future, I imagine that they're also seeing that there's a fifty percent chance of divorce. Are they doing anything to protect what they stand to lose in a divorce?

A striking characteristic of this generation of young men is that they want hands-on contact with their kids. In this year's student essays, more men than women gave specifics of what they would be doing with their kids in fifteen years. "I'm going to get the kids up in the morning, take them to school, practice Little League with them, help them with their homework." They anticipate hands-on contact. So men are moving toward more active participation in family life, and women are moving toward shared responsibility for breadwinning. That's healthy, both for parents and their children. In Paula Kamen's book *Feminist Fatale*, she interviewed young people in their twenties around the country, and she too found that the expectation was that they would both work, but the woman's career would step back to the duties of motherhood, while the man's career would be primary.

The use of the phrase "step back" and the alternate use of the word "primary" is interesting to me. If they're both interested in more hands-on involvement with the kids, I have to wonder who's really stepping back.

Men and women have the same needs to have a balance between an interesting career and access to their family. The studies show that the happiest people have both career and family. So I absolutely agree with you, that men have been hurt by the focus on overwork as their identity. It's bad for men's emotional and physical health. It's also bad for kids, because all the studies show that kids who have two involved parents do much better academically, have better social skills, and are even more empathetic, as I documented in *50-50 Parenting*. Kids need dads as much as moms.

The federal government passed the Family and Medical Leave Act in 1993 to provide unpaid parental leave. It's ostensibly gender neutral. In fact, will it be?

We already have a track record of employers that provide paternity leave; a tiny percentage of men take it. They're afraid that if they do, they'll not be considered serious workers, and their breadwinning role will be threatened.

What do we do about that?

Number one, we can establish national policy. The European Community has a formal recommendation to member countries to promote "increased participation by men in the care and upbringing of children."

Number two, we can learn from success. The Department of Water and Power in Los Angeles is a model. Besides parental leave, they have all kinds of other programs for fathers. I interviewed several DWP employees, including a father named George Fogelson. His whole fathering experience is different because of the parenting classes that he's taken at work. He said that without the added stimulus of the DWP parenting program, he might take a back seat in parenting.

DWP has a beeper program, so if your wife is expecting a baby and you're working in the field, and she goes into labor, you are paged. Fathers have four months' unpaid paternity leave. They have a fathers' section in their family resources library. They have a section about dads in their *Parents at Work* newsletter. They have a fathers' group that meets every month with a male facilitator. They organize "Daddy 'n' Me" weekend outings. On Father's Day they post pictures and let you match the dad with his kid. They have "DWP Dads Make a Difference" buttons. If every workplace had programs like that, fathers would know how important they are, not only as breadwinners, but as care-givers.

Who was the primary mover for the program at DWP and what was his motivation?

Her name is Beverly King. She's the head of DWP's Human Resources Division. Her motivation is that eighty percent of the employees are men, and many of them are dads.

How happy is she with the results of DWP's fathers program?

Very happy. It's saved them a lot of money in productivity, absenteeism, tardiness, retention and turnover. Most importantly, it increased employee satisfaction. As George Fogelson said, "It's a big plus as to why I'm staying here."

So why aren't more companies doing it?

Because we have a 1950s mentality that work and family are separate; you leave your family issues at home, you don't talk about them at work. Real men don't need to deal with these issues, because they're women's issues. It's our sense—since the nineteenth century—that family is feminine. It's the fact that the workplace is governed by men who have homemaker wives, and they don't "get" work and family issues. It's also because of the American ideal of rugged individualism. If you have a family issue, you don't ask for help. If you talk about it at work, it means you're a failure, you can't cope. It's our distrust of social solutions. We're ignorant about the workable solutions that exist here and in other countries, despite the studies that show cost savings in retention, productivity, et cetera. That's why I wrote *Empowering Parents*, to provide models of workplace, school and legislative programs.

Does this suggest that if the Clinton administration really wants to support families, and really wants to help achieve equality between men and women, then maybe it should look at the lessons of DWP and European countries and develop some sort of a national outreach program for men and fathers who want to take advantage of the Family and Medical Leave Act?

Yes. I think it has to start in the schools. The state of New York requires middle school students to take a home and career skills course. Starting in elementary school, there should be classes on life skills, where you learn how to parent and how to have a healthy relationship, how to communicate using "I" messages rather than "you" messages, where you learn conflict resolution and active listening. An example of a program for sixth graders is called "Oh, Boy, Babies!" They take the "coolest" sixth grade boys, and they let them push the babies around in strollers, and then everybody who wants to be "cool" wants to care for the babies. That way the boys don't grow up with that helpless sense of "Oh, my God, what do I do with this little baby?" They've handled babies and diapered them, and learned to feel comfortable with them.

I certainly agree with you, it would be great to start with kids, but can you see anything that the Clinton administration could do to make family leave gender neutral for men in the work force now?

Look at other countries. Sweden gives parents over a year of paid leave, including ten paid "New Daddy Days" right after a birth. Dads use time off to care for sick children as much as moms do. What the Swedes have talked about for years is to require that part of the extensive leave time be taken by a dad. Congress would never pass it, but ideally that would be great.

And of course the dad would be muttering under his breath, but smiling deep inside.

Guys in their twenties would not be muttering. They're looking forward to being hands-on fathers; it's a different attitude toward fathering now.

But even for guys in their twenties, family leave is not going to be gender neutral, is it?

No, because the corporation is still run by the old fraternity system, which means that if you're successful, your first love is the workplace. You can't have divided loyalties.

I want to take that same observation and put a different spin on it. I want to observe those old fraternity guys at the top, and suggest that what's on their minds is, "I didn't get to do that, buddy. And if I didn't get to do it, I don't see any reason why you should get to do it."

An example of that is the movie *Baby Boom* with Diane Keaton. Her boss says something like, "I don't even know my grandchildren's names," because he had to choose whether he was going to get to the top or spend time with his family.

So he's got all the power at the top, but he's got a big hole in his heart.

That's right. And that's why I think a lot of those men drink, and whatever else they do to fill their emptiness, like watch TV.

That raises another interesting issue about why family leave ought to be actually, instead of just technically, available to men. Are there any studies showing that employer costs for alcoholism and drug abuse go down when you have fathers who feel connected to their families?

It's proven that having a strong family-support system makes both men and women healthier and therefore more productive employees, and prevents burnout. Studies show that involved fathers have happier wives, which cuts down on stress, which cuts down on health costs to employers.

So just as a cold, rational, hard, bottom-line decision, it might make sense for corporations to look for ways to get men more connected with their families?

It's an historical aberration to remove men from family life. Our country did not begin on that foot. Men were very involved with their families in the rural-agrarian-colonial-frontier eras. The Protestant Reformation taught that the father was the priest of the family, responsible for his children's spiritual upbringing. It's only industrialism and capitalism that changed that level of involvement. Capitalism and the Industrial Revolution wanted men not to be too bonded to their families, so it could take them out of the home to the factories, so the home was redefined as a feminine realm.

I would agree that industrialism has been a problem, that materialism has been a problem. But do you think that in Soviet Russia, which didn't have capitalism, the economic system was any more friendly toward men?

Not to men as fathers. When Lenin was first in power, he tried to make steps toward equality, and free women from the burden of all the housework, but Stalin was reactionary and oppressive. Women were liberated to do paid work, but men weren't liberated to do family work.

> When I was in Russia, I was at a meeting of some people connected with family courts who had one of the most expansive maternity leave programs that I had ever seen—even more expansive than that of Scandinavia. When I asked them if they had paternity leave, (a) the translators thought I had made a mistake and couldn't translate, and (b) when they were corrected they all laughed and asked if in capitalist countries men give birth to babies.
>
> KAREN DeCROW
> former president of NOW
> keynote address to the National Congress for Men
> (now the National Congress for Men
> and Children)
> August 1982

So I would like to point the finger not so much at capitalism as much as at the materialistic idea that we have to produce, produce, produce and that men are the ones whose main purpose is to produce economically.

Yes. That's the crux of the problem. Men aren't supposed to get "soft."

Do you see any indication that some women might feel a little uncomfortable with the idea of the man gaining as much access to parenting opportunities as she has?

I've heard from women that it's hard to give up power at home if you don't have it anywhere else. Some very egalitarian mothers I've interviewed tell me that when their child is hurt and he or she runs to the father for comfort as readily as to the mother, there's a little pang over not being the one the child always goes to.

These women are especially egalitarian, they're on the forefront, and they are honest and aware enough to acknowledge that they feel a little pang. What do you think might be happening in the great heartland, where relationships are not so egalitarian?

We don't talk about it very much, but there are a lot of power and control issues in any relationship. I think that some women want control of the kitchen and nursery, and they do, on an unconscious level, shoo men away. What I hear that keeps men from being involved is that women impose their personal standards. Men tell me, "I dress the child and she says, 'Oh, she's too hot,' or I dress the child and, 'Oh, he's too cold.' " The natural reaction of any human being is to say, "Well, if I don't do it to your satisfaction, then you do it!" In terms of practical steps that women can take if they want men to be more involved in child rearing, I think it is necessary to keep their lips buttoned sometimes and not impose their particular standards. And they need to encourage men to spend time alone with their kids and develop their own style of parenting. Men and women have different styles; both are good, and kids need both.

One of the tragedies in this country today is that after divorce, fathers are not encouraged to stay involved with their kids. About a million kids each year experience divorce. Over thirty-five percent of American babies are born to unmarried mothers. Many fathers don't retain close contact with their children if the parents are not married. We don't talk about that enough. There needs to be a major push to keep men involved with kids, for the sake of our future as a nation.

> Recent research . . . challenges the popular assumption that non-custodial fathers of children born out of wedlock do not pay child support simply because they refuse to. Indeed, framing the discussion of delinquent child support payments in terms of "deadbeat dads" may oversimplify what is in fact a complex matter.
>
> "INSIGHTS"
> Institute for Research on Poverty
> University of Wisconsin
> March 1993

So maybe the government ought to be talking to so-called absent fathers about more than just how much child support they should pay.

The emphasis of the government, and often of the mothers, on financial support alone may deter many young fathers from seeking personal contact with their children.

Jacqueline Smollar, Ph.D., and
Theodora Ooms, MSW
"Young Unwed Fathers: Research Review, Policy
Dilemmas and Options"
funded by the Department of Health and
Human Services
October 1987

Yes. I think shared custody is vital, and so is counseling and mediation for divorcing parents. If you're feeling powerless, if you feel that you have no say, then a natural reaction is to turn away and not keep butting your head against a stone wall. I think we need to help mothers realize that if you don't want to see him, you can switch the children at school or child care. You don't have to see the father, but the kids need to see him, a lot.

Fathers are important to their children. The courts, employers and legislators need to act with that fact in mind.

Claudia Valeri

CLAUDIA VALERI, of Edmonton, Alberta, Canada, is the editor of *Reflections for Women*, a magazine of women's personal experiences. She started a radio-television career as one of the first female broadcasters at a radio station in Vancouver, British Columbia, and worked her way to a ten-year stint as a reporter with a Canadian TV network affiliate in Edmonton. She was divorced once, is now happily married, and has a daughter who was twenty months old at the time of our interview at the end of March 1993. Claudia was born in 1952.

Jack: *Let's get into "The Mission,"* * *the beautiful article you wrote in the current issue of* Reflections for Women. *Would you like to give a quick synopsis of what you were doing with that piece?*

Claudia: I had been very angry with my father for a long time. And angry with all men. I was one of those women who trashed men quite regularly. All men were wrong and everything was the fault of men. It was just in the last few years that I decided that I wanted to have a reconciliation with my father, not just for my father's sake, but for the sake of my marriage and for the sake of my

* Reprints available at no charge from Claudia Valeri, 11215 46 Avenue, Edmonton, Alberta T6H 0A2, Canada. Extra postage required for international mail; include international postage coupon or Canadian stamps with self-addressed envelope for reply.

family. If I ever have a son, I don't want him to grow up apologizing for being male. I knew in my heart I had to accept my father for the man he is. He did the best he could with the knowledge he had, and blaming him wasn't serving me or him.

The piece was based on something I did every Remembrance Day, which in Canada is the same as Veterans Day in the States. Wherever I was living, I would go to that city's war memorial. I didn't know why I felt compelled to be with the old World War II veterans, but then I realized I was searching for my father's spirit. My father had served proudly in the war. I finally realized that his spirit was a mystery that would very likely always remain a mystery to me, that there was something between men and women that is ineffable and unresolvable, and there's something very beautiful and natural about that.

I had been demanding that my father be more sensitive, that he tell me that he loved me, that he praise me more often, that he give me his blessing. This is a language that he doesn't know, he wasn't taught. I realized that my father loved me just by the way he lived his life. He provided for us, he put a roof over our heads. He gave every day of his life by working in a company job. I don't know how mind-numbing that was for my father, who was quite a courageous man. Giving all those days to his family was his expression of love.

I should point out I was raised in a family of girls. We had no brother and my mother was a full-time homemaker. So the whole idea of men was completely baffling to me. I just knew there was a very tall, loud man who brought the paycheck in every two weeks. He was not as effusive as my mother. I didn't understand him and I wanted his love more than anything in the world, but I didn't understand why he wouldn't give it to me in the way I wanted it.

Why would you want the love of this big, loud person who just brings home a paycheck every two weeks?

I don't know if it's a "why" question. I can only look at my husband with my daughter, and see something in that little girl's eyes when he comes to the door and she runs up to him and throws herself at him. It's not the same as the way she loves me. If I try to analyze it, I lose it. It's something very elusive. It's something very intangible. I don't know why I wanted his love. I just did. I wanted his blessing. I wanted him to admire me. I've heard sons talking this way about their fathers, too, and in some ways it's not that different. I wanted him to be proud of me.

Were you able to run up to your father the way your daughter is able to run up to your husband?

Yes. I don't want to present my father as an unfeeling block of cement. He wasn't verbal. He showed his affection through his actions. And now when I look at my father's actions—the way he read to us at bedtime, or took us to Stanley Park in Vancouver on a Sunday, or to the aquarium, or to the beach, and devoted an afternoon to playing with us—I know that was his love.

I don't want to generalize too much, but women love words and they love to hear the love and emotion expressed verbally. So I was hungry for something verbal, for him to say how much he loved us, how proud he was of us.

Were you verbally expressive of your love toward him?

No. While I was demanding an expression of love from my father, I was almost in a posture of having my arms folded across my chest, saying, "Well, come here and love me," without ever acknowledging him. So, another part of that piece I wrote about my father is that I don't think anyone in our family ever said thank you to him for what he did.

There probably is a lot of similarity here between sons and daughters in that regard. I never said thank you to my father. I don't think I ever did.

Then there was a lot of focus on what he *wasn't* to you?

Yes, definitely. And it's nice to think and talk about what he was. And I think perhaps lots of fathers right now are going to enjoy reading a recognition of what they are rather than only a critique of what they aren't.

Exactly. And maybe that's the start of reconciliation and healing: acceptance. Accepting someone doesn't mean they have no changes to make, or that they have no new ground to step out on. But to me the starting ground is acceptance.

The word that's in my mind, probably a sibling of acceptance, is appreciation.

Right.

If you were to translate your father's actions into words, what would they be?

"I give all I have to you. Everything I produce, I share this with you. This says I love you, that you're important to me and that you're important in my life. It's important that you receive what I give you, because what you're really receiving is my love. Please don't refuse it, because I am awkward and in pain about any other way to say this to you. I don't understand what you want from me, but this I can give."

My father just phoned me last night. He left the funniest message. He said, "I have your new phone number," even though I've had this phone number for months. He said, "I just put it on my computer, and it would be nice if you phoned." And then he just hung up. My husband didn't understand why I was really moved by that message. And I said, "That's Dad reaching out." It's very awkward and maybe even painful for him. And instead of correcting him and saying, "Why didn't you just say 'I miss you, give me a phone call?'" which I could do forever, I was just touched that he did what he did. My feeling is that, underneath, he was saying, "I miss you. Please call me." But it was underneath. The ruse was that he now had my new number on his computer. The electrical engineer just testing out the computer.

It's nice the way you're reading what your father was doing.

Well, I remember a couple of times when he did risk expressing his love to me. I had broken up with a boy when I was eighteen years old and I was in tears. He put his arm around me and I remember this distinctly. I took his arm and I threw it off my shoulder because I was mad at men. I don't think he ever put his arm around me again. Looking back, I can see nearly every time he risked opening up to us, we shut him down. I'm not being an apologist for him, but I am having some compassion for him.

We talked a little bit ago about how your disappointment with your father was generalized to all men. In the incident you just mentioned, disappointment with a man was transferred to your father.

Right. I never thought of that before.

I wonder if fathers sort of get it in both directions.

I think so. In fact, looking back, that's an excellent point. After my divorce, I believe I was more icy toward him than ever. I don't think I went to him for anything after my divorce. I had a female lawyer, and I went to my mother and my sisters, but I don't recall ever going to my father for any consolation. And I'm sure I shut him out of it. That's interesting.

He was an engineer? Did you get the impression he liked his work?

He was sometimes irritable when he came home. I had a sense he liked the engineering and scientific aspect of his work, but I don't know if he liked the office politics. I am just guessing here, but his sense of duty and honor compelled him to provide security and a steady paycheck at any cost, any personal cost. I just sense that the repetitious dullness of company life does something to the spirit of many men. Does that make sense to you?

It sure does.

That might make more sense to you than me. I was the recipient of it but I don't quite understand it.

As a young girl, did you think you understood it?

Yes.

What was your reading of it?

I was in continual judgment of him. I thought he was insensitive and selfish. My whole view of my father was how he treated *me*, instead of taking a step or two back to say, "What's going on with this man?"

Have you yet had the verbal communication with him that you would like to have?

I did tell him last year, for the first time, that I loved him. And it was pushing through a wall to say it. I kept wanting to run away from that wall, but I made a decision that I wanted to tell him before he died.

How did he respond?

He kissed me.

Did you get the feeling that it meant something to him?

Yes. In fact, I get emotional just thinking about it. He said he loved me too. I'm just guessing, but I felt like he had a weight lifted from his shoulders and so did I. One of the reasons I told him is because I remembered him telling me, "Before my father died, I told him I loved him." I kept thinking to myself, "I wonder if he's trying to tell me something." It was almost out of the blue. I took it as a cue: maybe he wants to know that before he dies. And I didn't think any more of it until a couple of years later.

So you're dealing with this wall between you and your father and it's a big, scary wall. And you want to run away from it but you managed to budge the gate open just enough to slip a note in there. And the note said, "I love you, Dad." If you could open up that gate wider, and know that your father would be glad to have it open, what more would you want to say?

Well, I tried to do it the easy way by writing that piece.

Has he read it?

Yes.

Did he say anything?

I have a sense that's what he phoned about. And of course, I'm terrified to hear what he has to say. After he read it, he did send a brief note and said he was just glad that someone was trying to understand his feelings.

He said that?

Yes, in a note. You asked me what would I say to him and you can see how I avoided answering. It would be really hard to say without being in tears. It would just be how much I love him, how much I've always looked up to him, how much his love means to me, how proud I am to be his daughter, how his love and respect for me is one of the most precious things in the world to me. Under all my anger and blame, when I get right down inside of me, that's what the truth really is. If I didn't feel that way about him, I wouldn't have been so angry all those years. I just wouldn't have cared.

Let's say that now he translates his actions into words. What would you like for him to talk with you about?

I would want to hear from him how much he loved me. I'd like to know how he felt about how I've pressed on in my own struggle, my own bravery, that he's proud of the fact that I've kept going, that I am a fighter, that he's been proud that I haven't quit in my life. Just that he loves me and he's proud of me. Those are the two main things. Anything else would flow out of those two.

The relationship a girl has with her father, even more than the one she maintains with her mother, can be the key to turning Daddy's little girl into the successful career woman of the future.

According to a study conducted at the Wright Institute of the University of California, Berkeley, college-age women who were encouraged by their fathers to be competent, to value their accomplishments, and to explore the world outside the home are likely to have high levels of self-esteem and independence. The study also shows that to achieve a high degree of self-confidence, a woman should identify not only with the traditional female role in our society but also with the male role.

Some would expect that encouragement of this sort would draw a daughter away from her mother. However, the study found that women who were given such stimulating treatment were close not only to their fathers but to their mothers as well.

MYRON BRENTON
Emotional Health

If you could imagine your father saying, "Claudia, I love you and I'm proud of you," does that feel different from imagining your mother saying, "Claudia, I love you and I'm proud of you."

Yes.

How so?

With my mother, it's more multistranded. That's the only way I can put it. It touches on who I am as a wife, as a mother, as a sister, as a daughter, as a writer. With my father, it's very simple and bottom-line. With my father it might be one sentence. With my mother it might be an essay. And it would say the same thing.

With your father the sentence would be, "I am proud of you as a . . ." what?

Boy, this is tough for some reason. "As a daughter of mine." That in some ways I won't be carrying on as a son would, carrying on everything that was passed down to him from father to son, father to son, but that I love and respect him, and that I will pass that on in honoring his integrity and living with honor and integrity in my life. I won't live my life like he did, because I'm not the same person, but I'll respect and carry on the best parts of him, and honor his memory.

A few minutes ago you talked about how your disappointment and anger toward your father were the sad aspect of what was really your love for your father.

Right.

And we've talked about how some of your feelings for your father have been projected out to all men, and how some of your feelings for men have been projected back to your father. Do you think that perhaps much of the criticism of men that we see happening in the world today is really a sad manifestation of women's love for men?

Yes. I think a lot of that anger manifests as "open season" on men. You see and hear it on most TV talk shows. In my opinion, trashing men is a deep cry of despair from the feminine heart to be loved and to express love. In my own experience, the anger masks a fear of being vulnerable again and fully opening up and giving a hundred percent of myself emotionally and spiritually to a man in my life. The anger masks a fear that if I do that again I'll go back to the way it was in the 1950s, so I'll be powerless again or I'll be a victim again, or I'll be used again. It becomes a no-win situation. The trashing of men and the anger expressed toward men has not advanced me any further toward what I want in my life than being powerless in the fifties did. What I really want is to have a relationship with a man where I can be all of me, where everything is fully expressed and felt, where we're in each other's lives for our mutual fulfillment, where he's free to dream his dreams and sometimes that changes every year. And likewise with me. I just feel a lot of the anger is masking a fear of not getting what women's hearts are really aching for with men.

Does that mean that the man must be verbally expressive of his emotions in order to be emotionally intimate?

There's room for him to do it in his own way. My husband and I went on a retreat for couples about two months ago, and the biggest discovery I made was I need to allow my husband to love me in the way he wants to love me. It doesn't mean placing demands on him and it doesn't mean dictating to him how he should express himself. And the irony is that the minute I took all those controls and rules away from him, the demands away from him, he felt safer than ever to come more than halfway toward me and fully express everything in his heart to me.

And when he felt safe to meet you at least halfway and express what was in his heart, did you find paradoxically that he became more verbal?

Yes. That's very true. And I became quieter. And when I actually stopped and listened to my husband, I couldn't believe how I hadn't heard him all these years. I had been demanding that he speak to me in a certain way which was more like the way women speak, rather than in a man's own authentic voice.

Ruth Shalit

RUTH SHALIT is a reporter covering politics and cultural issues for *The New Republic* magazine, based in Washington, D.C. She graduated Phi Beta Kappa from Princeton University in June 1992 with a degree in history and European cultural studies. In the July 1992 edition of *Reason* magazine, she analyzed a false accusation of rape occurring at her alma mater. She was born in 1970.

Jack: *Can you give us the essentials of Princeton's Take Back the Night demonstration in the spring of 1991?*

Ruth: First of all, I want to say that I don't oppose the goal of the Take Back the Night march at Princeton or at any other school. The goal is to promote awareness about rape and to help women develop skills for protecting themselves. In the past, the marchers agitated for better campus lighting, self-defense courses, and so on. Rape is a horrible crime; it should be decried, and women should know how to protect themselves against it.

But over the past couple of years, the march has been hijacked by a group of activist feminists whose goals are radical and millennial. Under their leadership, the march has promoted acrimony between men and women on campus.

Every year, there's a fresh debate over whether men should be allowed to march. Usually the men lose out. The women who plan the march have said, "No, men are not allowed to march; they're the oppressors, they're what we're marching against." There's no distinction between the sins of individual males and the male sex as a whole. Males are regularly denounced as the oppressor class, and rape is presented as white-male business-as-usual.

At the end of the march, the victims are shuffled onto a stage and handed microphones and they're told that not only does their testimony have personal and therapeutic value for the listeners, but it has political value as well. By coming forward, they're helping to raise consciousness about male oppression.

Instead of recounting the specifics of what happened to them, the victims began to ideologize their stories. They began to say not just "This happened to me, and here's what you can do to make sure this doesn't happen to you," but were encouraged by the campus Women's Center activists who ran the march to say, "This happened to me, and it shows why all male-female interaction is just another structure of oppression."

So, what happened in the spring of 1991 was inevitable.

A woman got up to speak and accused a fellow student of raping her. She described a crime that was almost gothically brutal. She said that this guy dragged her to his room and tied her up. While raping her, he screamed things like, "My father buys me cheap girls like you to use up and throw away," and "public school bitch." He banged her head against the headboard until she was unconscious, and then dumped her at the entry to her dorm.

She didn't originally name a particular guy, did she?

No, she just said it was a student, a male student on campus. She said that after he raped her, she filed a complaint with the dean of students office, and the student agreed to withdraw for a year, but that he was now back on campus. She said he belonged to her eating club, so she saw him every day, and it was terribly disempowering for her to see this student and to know that no real action was taken against him.

She got so caught up in her story that she submitted a written version to *The Daily Princetonian,* the student paper. The dean of students saw it and said, "Hey, wait a minute. This woman is maligning the dean of students office; she's saying that we failed to respond adequately to her complaint. I don't want women who are raped to be afraid to come and talk to us." So he wrote a letter explaining that if this had really happened, the male student would have been disciplined very severely. He would not have been allowed to remain in the community.

And rather than retract her story, she escalated it?

Exactly. We can never know what was going through her head, but apparently her peers approached her and said, "Hey, what's going on? Dean Lowe said you never filed a complaint." She went on to name a particular student, spreading his name around campus. She had to escalate it into this huge conspiracy theory, and a web of deceit leading all the way up to the university president's office. Later, she admitted she had never even met or spoken to the guy she accused. Finally he was forced to bring a complaint of sexual harassment against her.

What happened with his sexual harassment claim?

The details of the arrangement worked out in the dean of students office were kept confidential. They obviously reached some kind of settlement. Part of the settlement was a retraction of her story. It appeared on the op-ed page of *The Daily Princetonian* on the last publication day of the semester. Her defense was, "I was overcome by emotion."

Even after her retraction, she was supported by the Women's Center activists who said, "Listen, we cannot hope to find truth in all these stories. The goal is to reveal these women as 'lenses of oppression' through which the crimes of the patriarchy can be exposed." So you have the act of rape expanded into a metaphor for all male-female relations. Rape victims in this society have enough trouble getting taken seriously, without this kind of thing.

> Ginny, a college senior who was really raped when she was 16, suggests that false accusations of rape can serve a useful purpose. . . . In her view, rape is a subjective term, one that women must use to draw attention to other, nonviolent, even nonsexual forms of oppression. "If a woman did falsely accuse a man of rape, she may have had reasons to."
> Catherine Comins, assistant dean of student life at Vassar . . . argues that men who are unjustly accused can sometimes gain from the experience. . . . "I think it ideally initiates a process of self-

exploration. 'How do I see women?' 'If I didn't violate her, could I
have?' 'Do I have the potential to do to her what they say I did?'
Those are good questions."

NANCY GIBBS
Time
June 3, 1991

*Take Back the Night started out as an effort to help women, but it
became something else. What is its purpose now?*

I think part of the design is to make men feel excluded. Make
them feel guilt-ridden, and to categorize the male as the oppressor
class whose only purpose is to marginalize and victimize women.

What designs do these women have for men in their ideal world?

They want relations between the sexes relegated to a quasi-
legalistic, quasi-contractual realm. For a guy and girl to get together, consent has to be as explicit as a legal contract. I know
men who keep tape recorders under their beds to protect themselves from false accusations. This is one of the few socio-political
changes that's actually affected my own life, and the lives of my
friends.

At the University of California at Berkeley, . . . the coordinator
of the Rape Prevention Education Program insists that according to
what she sees on a campus of more than 25,000 students, one
woman in four stands a chance of being raped. Yet only two rapes
were reported there last year. What accounts for the disparity . . . ?
[T]he answer now given is that sexually violated students are . . .
simply unaware that [rape] occurred.

NEIL GILBERT
professor of social welfare
University of California at Berkeley
in an op-ed piece published in the
Wall Street Journal
June 27, 1991

Men are running scared. They really are. It was hard enough before to get men to make a pass at you, and now it's much harder, because they're afraid they're going to be slapped with a lawsuit. And even in the bedroom, it's the same thing. You can murmur a half-protesting no, and his hands will just fly off you. And you can't say, "Wait," because feminist sexual politics leaves no room for equivocations and murmurings.

You said it was hard enough to get men to make passes at you. Perhaps one thing that ought to happen is that women should begin to make more passes of their own?

I think that would be a good start. I think it's hard for some of us.

Getting through Princeton was hard for some of you. Getting a job at The New Republic *was hard for some of you.*

I think this is all sort of a personal thing. The problem with contemporary feminism is that it tries to ideologize personal and emotional issues that are not necessarily amenable to a political or quasi-legal resolution.

Tell me how you try to get men to make passes at you.

It's subliminal and visual. It's not verbal. You have all these little tricks. I remember in school, when the guy you liked was sitting behind you, a friend and I would touch our neck, play with our neck, because we heard that drove guys crazy, just necks. Things like that.

What were you hoping the guy would do when you touched your neck?

Dip my braid in the inkwell? I don't know. Fall in love with me, I guess.

Do men ever respond awkwardly?

Yes. I think we've gotten to the point where we're vilifying men for making what amount to botched passes.

I can't help observing that what women do is very safe. Nobody has ever gotten in trouble for a botched neck touch.

Women are granted a lot more leeway. And also—I think this is psychological and biological, rather than just cultural—I think female expression tends to be more subliminal, more oblique, whereas men tend to be linear and straightforward. It's definitely the male of the species who is biologically and culturally programmed to go out on a limb.

Some could argue that the female of the species was biologically and culturally programmed to sit at home and take care of kids. But women have rejected sitting home if they don't want to. Wouldn't it be a good idea, now that we're concerned about making things fair and equal and better between men and women, for women to do other things that go against their biological and cultural programming . . .?

And be more aggressive?

Aggressive would be one word we could use . . .

But you think that's pejorative. More direct.

More active; less passive. What's the first cousin of victimhood? Passivity.

Passivity, yes. That was my problem with the politics of Take Back the Night and the rhetoric of victimhood that institutionalizes the stereotype of woman as passive.

The whole female sexual idiom is passive, isn't it? Wouldn't most guys say that women seldom . . .

Take the initiative?

Take the initiative, take the risk, put themselves out?

Well, it depends what the context is. There are certain rituals that men have traditionally initiated. Asking the woman out for a date. The first date.

But there are lots of traditions we've recognized aren't helpful. Tradition would be one word; somebody else could call it reactionary. Somebody else might call it Neanderthal. It's traditional; people do it. People have done it for a long time. Does that mean we want to keep doing it?

I think that women should just go with the flow. Not to string together clichés, but whatever floats your boat. If it makes you comfortable, then by all means, go for it.

If men did only what was comfortable for them, sexual relations would come to a grinding halt.

That's an interesting point.

I think there's a direct connection between women's failure to initiate and sexual harassment, which, after all, is just men's failure to initiate well.

That's a big question. I think of myself as a strong ambitious woman who's willing to work hard to get what she wants. So why can't I translate that kind of bird-dog relentlessness and ferocity into the realm of romantic and sexual attraction? I don't know.

I would suggest that the reason is precisely because—in the short term only—you maximize your power by controlling the transaction. The person who expresses the need is the person who is in the weaker bargaining position. It's precisely because you're a powerful woman, who likes being powerful, that you're not about to get down on one knee and say, "Excuse me, would you go out with me?" Like the feminists say, "Nobody gives up power willingly." But we need to look beyond short-term power.

I'll think about that.

You were talking about the marchers' idea that rape is a metaphor for men's subjugation of women.

> No one cares what the real numbers are, they just want to make political statements.
>
> Kathryn Newcomer
> professor of statistics and public policy at George Washington University
> commenting on a bogus but widely reported "study" of the incidence of rape
> *Insight*
> January 28, 1991

Yes. In the act of rape all men's evils are sort of condensed and expressed.

What could we say then about what a false accusation of rape is, from women to men?

I think it's a compelling metaphor for women's oppression of men, under the guise of social equity and other progressive concerns.

I want you to tell me—because I'm sure that's the remaining element of the story that we haven't gotten to yet—about the march the men had after the false accusation was revealed. It was probably called Take Back the Truth, right?

There was no march.

What did the men do?

They didn't do anything. The problem may be the lack of a men's movement. There's no Men's Center; there's no men's studies program. There's no locus for this kind of activity.

Let's explore whether there's even any impulse for this kind of activity. Did you talk to any of your men friends at Princeton about the false accusation?

Oh, yeah, I mean, all sensible people at Princeton, sensible men and women, obviously condemned the false accusation.

What were the men's reactions?

Bemusement and frustration that this had proceeded as far as it had. Anger. A lot of anger. Empathy for the guy who had been falsely accused. It hit most of the guys I talked to on a personal level. There was a real feeling of violation, a sort of visceral outrage.

What do you mean by bemusement?

I mean that they were annoyed by it, but at the same time, there was this kind of effort to ironically distance themselves from the whole thing.

Anything like denial?

Yes, a lot of denial, actually. But at the same time, working against the denial there was, as I said, a tremendous amount of empathy and sympathy for the guy.

It would seem that if you took a bunch of healthy, red-blooded American men, seventeen to twenty-one years old, and you stirred up frustration, anger, empathy and visceral outrage . . .

You've got a pretty potent mixture.

Perfect word; that's the perfect word. And then on the other hand, because of denial, we have the opposite of potent.

I think that's right.

Do they know? Do they know they're impotent?

Women taking a class in feminist art at the University of Maryland publicly labeled male students whose names they picked from a campus phone book as "potential rapists" . . . on hundreds of posters put up around campus. . . . The women who put up the posters said every identifiable male name in the student directory was put on the list . . .

Women involved in the project asked to remain anonymous, fearing harassment . . .

ASSOCIATED PRESS
May 7, 1993

I think there's a lot of denial. I think that when something awful and unfair happens to a woman, there's a rush of support, and if you don't support the woman, you're perceived as being unsisterly. But I think that the male community is much more atomized. There's not the same sense of group identification.

What keeps men atomized?

I think identity politics is very problematic. I think you gain something by subsuming your will under the prerogative of NOW or Take Back the Night or another one of these female mass movements, but I think you lose a lot, too. I think there's a sense that what's individual in you is being stamped out. And so I think that a lot of men have seen that happening, and I don't think they want it to happen to them.

One of the great things about the American personality is rugged individualism. But that can be taken to an extreme. Divide and conquer would be perhaps the best statement of how it can be harmful. At the risk of being politically incorrect, I'll use some imagery I think readers will understand. When the rugged American individualists were driving their wagon trains across the prairie, and the Apaches attacked, the pioneers circled the wagons. But it seems that this wagon train of men in the 1990s just keeps plugging along to Oregon, and saying, "Arrows? What arrows?"

It's like the Poles in '39. "I don't see any Luftwaffe. The sky looks clear to me."

I think that seeking group solace, group empowerment, even if it's empowerment of a specifically political, as opposed to therapeutic, nature, is perceived as somehow emasculating. And I think that that's too bad.

Do you think that the wagon drivers who circled the wagons felt emasculated because they circled the wagons and helped each other out? Do you think that when the posse got together to track down the bad guy, they felt emasculated?

No, and when somebody throws a long pass to somebody else on the other side of the field, do they feel emasculated? No. Some rituals are perceived as culturally acceptable; some are not. The idea that males need empowerment has always been sort of suspect.

Something seems very twisted when the act of males taking power is seen as disempowering. What's suspect about it?

Men's groups have come under fire from women's groups, who've said, "Look, we're the victims, damn it, you guys."

Have you seen men's groups come under fire also from men?

Yes, but not with the same kind of heated political attack. It's more of a scorn and derision.

You talked earlier about making men feel guilt-ridden. Do you think men are feeling guilty about being male? Are they feeling shamed about being male?

Absolutely. I think that the curricula being advanced on college campuses are designed to promote that. I think that that's a very real problem.

If a guy were to stand up on campus, and were to start distributing flyers saying, "There is going to be a rally tomorrow night in front of the Student Union to focus attention on the position in which men find themselves," what would your personal reaction be to that guy?

I would think that he was really ballsy. I would be shocked first of all at the sight of males noisily empowering themselves. It's just not something you're used to seeing.

I think if a male were falsely accused by a vindictive professor of cheating on a test, and if he then tried to turn his plight into a symbol of oppression of all males, I think that would be fatuous. But I think the plight of the student at Princeton reflects the degenerated state of sexual politics on campus, and more broadly in our country. I think that this has got to stop.

Suzanne Steinmetz

In 1974, SUZANNE STEINMETZ, Ph.D., coedited a book entitled *Violence in the Family* and contributed a chapter called "Male Liberation—Destroying the Stereotypes" to a book entitled *The Process of Relationships*. In 1975 she was one of the primary researchers on the National Family Violence Survey funded by the National Institutes of Mental Health. Also in 1975 she completed her doctoral dissertation, which was later published as *The Cycle of Violence*. From the data compiled for her dissertation and several smaller studies, she published an article called "The Battered Husband Syndrome" in *Victimology*, a scholarly journal, in 1978. She is now the chair of the Sociology Department and director of the Family Research Institute at Indiana University/Purdue University in Indianapolis.

Jack: *Could you describe what you found in your dissertation data?*

Suzanne: In my dissertation as well as studies based on data collected from students in a number of countries, I looked at violence between husbands and wives, but I analyzed the data as couple data, without distinguishing who was violent, the husband or the wife. A number of colleagues asked, "How much of the couple violence is really husband-to-wife violence?" To my amazement, I discovered that the husband-to-wife and wife-to-husband violence were virtually equal.

When you discovered that, did you begin to doubt your research?

No. I read the literature to see if there was anything that could account for what I had found. That's when I discovered that quite a lot had been written about the acceptability of women using violence on men. Historically, men who were abused by their wives were ridiculed as if there was something wrong with them because they could not protect themselves.

Battered men were publicly humiliated. For example, in France in the 1700s, they were blindfolded and made to ride a donkey backwards through the streets while holding the donkey's tail. They were made fools of because they had not lived up to expectations of masculinity.

Your findings must have upset the worldview held by a lot of people. Were you criticized for publishing your article on battered husbands?

Yes. For instance, after the article was published, I was scheduled to give a speech sponsored by the American Civil Liberties Union in Richmond, Virginia. The woman in charge called to let me know that they had received a bomb threat and that they were going to have police at the speech, but they didn't think anything would happen. And nothing did happen. Fortunately, it was all hot air. At the same time, I was getting calls at home from women saying, "If you don't stop talking about battered men, something's going to happen to your children and it won't be safe for you to go out." I think they were driven by their fear that attention might be diverted from wife abuse. They certainly had not thought clearly about the implications of their threats. I thought it was really ironic that they were threatening to use violence to stop me from speaking about women's potential to be violent. From their perspective, there was no such thing as a battered man—women just were not violent. Years after I had been promoted, I learned that this group of women had contacted female faculty at the university where I was employed and urged the women to work against me for promotion and tenure.

The findings were pretty much the same ten years later in the 1985 National Family Violence Survey, weren't they?

Yes. They found pretty much the same thing about husbands and wives. They looked at levels of injury, too, and found very little difference there, either. They also found that wife abuse overall had decreased rather dramatically, while abuse against husbands showed virtually no decrease and in certain categories actually went up. The researchers surmised that as you increase education and awareness and provide resources, people change their ways. Since the most effort had been expended in reducing child abuse, it was not surprising that there was nearly a fifty percent decrease in reported abuse between 1975 and 1985. Somewhat less effort had been spent on wife-abuse prevention and intervention, and the study found nearly a thirty percent decrease. Unfortunately, there had been little increase of services for battered men during this period.

It is important to pay attention to violence against men for two reasons that might not be obvious. First, you cannot hope to eliminate family violence until you approach it from all sides. Second, by ignoring or devaluing women's violence toward men, we are saying to women that it doesn't matter what they do. Their actions are of no consequence, even if these actions are disturbing to them. In the end women are losers, too. There are a variety of programs for men who are violent. Not only are programs and support groups lacking for violent women, these women are made to believe that the problem lies in their head—they are imagining that they are violent. They are left trying to figure out how to deal with their own tempers and being out of control without support and resources. Even more disturbing, they are made to feel that they are alone in experiencing this problem. I have had women tell me that they call shelters and other services and explain that they are feeling out of control, have been slugging their husbands, do not like feeling this way and need some help. They're essentially told, "Oh, you can't do him any harm. Don't worry about it"—statements that devalue their concerns and fears. I think we ought to be more humane than that.

What do you think of that idea, that you can't do him any harm and don't worry about it?

Well, the bottom line is: yes, she can.

Can you describe some of the ways in which women can injure men?

The same ways that men can injure women.

What I want you to address is the idea that since men are bigger . . .

When you use weapons you equalize brute force. A woman with a weapon can do as much damage as a man with a weapon or a child with a weapon. In hitting, slapping, shoving and kicking, women typically don't do quite as much damage, because they aren't as big. But with weapons it's about equal.

Why are men not speaking up about their problem?

I think they are, more and more.

You think that this issue is becoming more and more recognized?

Oh, yes. And I've been told that the courts are now listening to the other side. It's going to be slow. It took a long time for us to recognize that there was child abuse and wife abuse, so it's going to take time to recognize husband abuse. But there are men's groups that provide support. They deal with men's issues in general, and I think they are serving as a source of support and help for these men. Also the courts and the police are becoming a little more sophisticated.

How do we know that women's violence is not simply in reaction to men's violence?

The people who say that women's violence is only in reaction to men's violence look at the statistics and say, "Well, it looks like the women who battered were battered first, they battered men in retaliation." That's not true. Both National Family Violence Surveys show that in about half the families who use violence, both individuals had used violence, although it is not possible to ascertain whether the violence occurred during the same incident. In the remaining half, one fourth were men who had used violence against wives, and the wives had never used violence. One fourth were women who had used violence against husbands, and the husbands had never used violence.

We need to recognize that just as some men are violent, some women are also violent. In some families you have mutually violent interactions—"She throws, he hits." In other families, both partners use violence, but the wife may use violence in one interaction, the husband may use violence in another. It is important to recognize that even when both partners had reported using violence, we do not know whether both used violence in a single,

reciprocating incident, or in different incidents possibly in retaliation for earlier altercations.

But the skeptics say that if a woman hits it's only because . . .

I think that the causes of women's violence are very similar to
the factors that produce men's violence: inadequate resources,
stress, lack of the ability to properly care for one's family, frustration, substance abuse, and unemployment. When we looked at
these factors twenty-five years ago, we saw them as the reason why
men were frustrated and lashed out. Now virtually every woman has
to work. Stress and rates of alcoholism among women are increas-
ing. Women lose their jobs or have a problem on the job, they
come home and take it out on the family. These are the same
indicators we saw with men. Equality has its down side, you know.

*In some of the literature I read from the domestic violence activists,
there seems to be an undertone of a belief that men are inherently violent.
That they are inherently morally inferior to women. Have you detected
this?*

No, I haven't detected that. The literature that I'm aware of
would indicate that men under certain circumstances have the pre-
disposition to be more violent because of testosterone. And of
course, we're all aware of the literature about men from certain social
classes or certain generations who were expected to fight to show
they were real men. Those are the only two trends that I've seen.

What do you make of the testosterone component of the problem?

The literature is mixed. The problem is that for every male-
related hormonal or genetic problem, you can find a female parallel.
Pre-Menstrual Syndrome or menopause, for example. So I don't
know that anybody has actually tried to come up with an accurate
rating of which gender's hormones cause the most havoc. But the
bottom line is that the prevailing social norms create an environment where violence is either accepted or not.

*Do you have any sense that the domestic violence facts are being
obscured, denied or distorted by those who have a political agenda that is
disserved by publication of the facts?*

Yes, but I don't believe it is limited to domestic violence activists.
As an advocate, you select those data which support the point you're

trying to make. For example, Indianapolis doesn't have a major gang problem when compared to other large cities. Nevertheless, one can use statistics to present a picture of growing gang-related activities and the need to obtain resources to alleviate the problem. A similar phenomenon occurs when activists advocate for resources for abused women. There is the fear that if you documented that husbands and wives were equally violent, legislators might assume that these violent husbands and wives were partners and could easily take care of themselves. The fear results from the fact that there are so few resources available to address so many needs.

Domestic violence against men is just not a social problem.

ELLEN PENCE
founder of the Domestic Abuse Intervention Project
Duluth, Minnesota
quoted by Tamar Lewin in the *New York Times*
April 20, 1992

I see activists from the domestic violence "community" who use what I would call distortions of domestic violence data to oppose what I would call advances in the law, efforts to make the law more equal in ways in which it's been unequal to the detriment of men.

Could you give me an example? I'm not sure what you mean.

Divorce reform. They say joint custody of children is a bad idea because men will only use joint custody as a way of maintaining their access to the woman so that they can beat her up.

Joint custody opponents raise the specters of spouse abuse and suspect motivations (usually on the part of the father requesting joint custody) as evidence that joint custody is dangerous to women's interests.

"Synopses of Sole and Joint Custody Statutes"
Report R103A
Children's Rights Council
Washington, D.C.

I am not aware of that argument.

And what I'm suggesting is that when fathers' groups ask for more contact with their kids, women's activists are saying "No, no, no, men are violent." Phyllis Chesler, for instance, wrote Mothers on Trial, *a book in which she claims that sixty-two percent of fathers who won custody "had physically abused their wives during marriage or divorce."*

Dr. Chesler studied a unique group of mothers and fathers. It doesn't make sense to generalize her findings to all men and women who are attempting to gain custody. In the past several decades, fathers have been taking a more active role in child care. It's not unreasonable to expect that close fathering relationships will continue after divorce. Custody battles bring out the worst in parents.

Why do nonviolent men stay in abusive relationships?

Their reasons are similar to those given by women. They hope that the violence will subside. They are attached to their home, community and family. They believe that a two-parent home will be better and they are concerned that if they leave, the mother may become violent toward the children. Sometimes they do leave and then they try to fight for custody of their children.

Do men sometimes stay because they're afraid they are not going to win custody of their children?

Yes, definitely. No question about that.

Could you describe the flaws that exist in surveys and studies using shelter populations and police reports as their data bases?

The shelter populations are biased because they are based on a very skewed sample of women—those who are battered and have nowhere else to go or anyone else to turn to. They only represent those battered women who go to shelters—not all women in general.

And what's the flaw with police reports?

Because of the macho image, men tend not to report the incident unless they end up in the emergency room. But women, possibly because they hope that the police might prevent further violence, are more inclined to report lesser levels of violence. A woman who has a black eye suffers a lot of stigma and embarrassment when she reports that her husband did it, but there's even more embarrassment and stigma for the man who has to admit that the "little woman" did this to him.

Is there an analogy between men's reluctance to report domestic violence and women's reluctance to report crimes upon them, for instance, rape perhaps?

That's a good observation. In both instances there is embarrassment, stigma and the belief that the victim was somehow responsible for the violence. The woman who was raped is assumed to have been in the wrong place, at the wrong time, wearing the wrong clothes. The man who is battered is assumed to have provoked the incident or been hit in retaliation for abusing the woman. Both sets of assumptions are wrong.

How could a more realistic and holistic approach to domestic violence benefit everyone in the long run?

Indianapolis is doing something that I think might be a model for the country. They have consolidated all domestic violence-related agencies for child abuse, elder abuse, marital abuse under one agency—called Family Advocacy—which provides a range of services. They don't look at the problem as battered women, abused children, elder abuse. They view it as a family problem and provide services to the entire family. It's a more comprehensive approach that is much more likely to reduce family violence.

I have a mother. I have two sisters. I have nieces. I have women friends. And I care about them. For that reason I should be very interested in working to put a stop to domestic violence. And in my own way, I am. But I find myself not interested in plugging into the agencies and organizations working on domestic violence, because I feel that their approach is degrading to me, to me as a man, because their analysis of the problem is that it's a masculine thing. It's a male thing. And by cooperating with the agencies, I'm only helping to call attention to these people's belief that domestic violence is connected to being male. I wish I didn't feel this way, but I feel that the activists are interested in two things. One, they are interested in helping women. Two, they're interested in hurting men.

> As the beer cooled and the testosterone surged . . . , a network
> of feminist activists orchestrated a national campaign to ask males to
> stop beating their wives and girlfriends after the Super Bowl. . . .
> Despite their dramatic claims, none of the activists appears
> to have any evidence that a link actually exists between football
> and wife-beating. Yet the concept has gained such credence that
> their campaign has rolled on anyway, unabated. Last week it
> produced . . . a public relations mailing . . . warning at-risk women:
> "Don't remain alone with him during the game."
>
> KEN RINGLE
> *Washington Post*
> January 31, 1993

I have a husband, two sons, a son-in-law and three grandsons.
I'm concerned that women not be abused, and I'm equally concerned that all men not be maligned for the deeds of some. I'm not
aware of activists' attempts to deliberately hurt men, but I am aware
of attempts to further the cause of women by not presenting the
entire picture. Unfortunately, when political rhetoric takes prece-
dence over service delivery, everyone loses.

*If you were to come across someone who suggested that women are
inherently more peaceful and loving . . .*

Oh, that's not true. Margaret Mead showed us that over fifty
years ago in her early study of gender. In one society the males were
very aggressive and the females were submissive. In another society,
they were both very peaceful and there was no violence at all. In a
third society they were both incredibly aggressive and violent. We
all have the innate ability to be violent or nonviolent. It's our
socialization that makes the difference. If we live in a society that
tells us to be violent, provides the instruction on how to be violent,
rewards us for violence under the right circumstances—for example, the military or certain sports—then we're going to be violent.

*Inside the family, violence is about equal between men and women,
but outside the family men are much more violent. Why does society
want men to be that way?*

Because it's the aggressive bastard who wins. It's the hard player
who wins. It's not the sweet, loving "oh, just do whatever you

want" kind of guy who ends up as the head of corporations. Being aggressive means taking risks, getting ahead, not letting anyone stand in your way. This is how the West was won, how World War II was won and how you move up the corporate ladder. Mr. Milquetoast does not move up the corporate ladder. Mr. Nice Guy is not a hero. You get ahead by taking risks, doing your fellow workers in. Furthermore, violent acts among young women, both individual acts and gang-related violence, are skyrocketing. It is possible that in the future women will be equally as violent as men outside the home, too.

Could it be that one of the things that helps to make men crazy is that the qualities that we're loved for, the qualities that win us love—being aggressive and competitive and willing to kick butt and take names—are also the qualities for which we're hated?

You've got it. That's true. I never thought of it that way. That's right, and the same thing happens with women. We admire the woman who gets ahead, but we'll call her aggressive, a bitch, frigid.

We've seen some analyses of why men beat up women. Men are taught to treat women as property. Men are taught that they should be in control of their women. I wonder what is the dynamic that's operating on women to cause them to be violent to their husbands.

I think women see men as their major support. Many of the women who abuse their husbands are also economically dependent. It's very important that her husband behave a certain way, because that's her livelihood, and deviation from the ideal is very threatening. Typically, men are beaten up because they came home late, the woman suspected he was out drinking or was with another woman. In my research, a woman's violence is often tied to jealousy and possessiveness. From a woman's perspective, if that man leaves her, she's in trouble. So, of course, she's going to do everything possible to hold onto him. That's not too different from the man who views his wife as property, and will beat her up or kill her to keep her from leaving him.

Are there any other points you think we should make?

I hope that your book isn't seen as one side versus another side. I hope it stresses the importance of looking at violence between family members as *family* violence, because as long as we allow any group to divide participants into abused children versus abused elderly, or abused wives versus abused husbands when providing services, *family* violence will not be conquered.

Unless we address violence in the family we are going to continue to have violence in the streets.

Attorney General Janet Reno
at her Senate confirmation hearings
March 9, 1993

Audrey B. Chapman

AUDREY CHAPMAN is nationally known as an expert on black male-female relationships. She is a Washington, D.C., therapist who specializes in family and relationship issues and has a private practice working with groups, married couples and single couples. On Howard University's radio station, WHUR, she hosts a call-in show called *All About Love*. She is at work on *Entitled to Good Lovin': The Black Battle for Power and Passion*, a book scheduled for publication in 1994.

Jack: *Do you think that African-American men need and would appreciate some expressions of good will toward them?*

Audrey: There's no doubt about it. I think that in general African-American men perceive that black women don't have much that's good to say about them. Many black women are very angry because they are often left on their own to deal with the ups and downs of daily living, and because it seems so difficult to love black men.

Black women often say that black men come to them because of what they—the men—need, and that it is very difficult for the men to provide what the women need. Black women want to be held, respected and loved by black men. Black men also want the same in return. Both groups feel the other individual owes them what they've not received throughout life. I have described this dynamic as the Entitlement Syndrome. Black men and women believe that they are owed what they feel they've not been given by society and their families. Whether that's justified or not doesn't matter; it has had a grave impact on the way black men and women have related to each other. This attitude has funneled down into their relationships with each other. The woman has expectations, and her expectations of the man are often greater than he could possibly supply. That leaves her disappointed and angry, feeling abandoned and uncared about. Then she acts all that out. by behaving in an indifferent way to him. "I don't need you." That's a problem. You can pick up any book on marriage and relationships and learn that the core of a balanced relationship is interdependence, not independence or dependence.

I've heard it said that "black mothers raise their daughters and love their sons." What's that about?

Ever since slavery, black women have been assigned the role of protecting black men in this society. The women had to watch the men be beaten and sometimes hung. So they began to groom their young sons to be more docile, less outright, less aggressive, less outspoken and more childlike so that they would be less of a threat to white males, basically. That way the mother felt that she was keeping her boy child safe. Some slave women, of course, also experienced terribly cruel things, but they didn't have to worry as much about being killed as men did. More often they were raped and beaten.

How did this inability to protect their loved ones affect black fathers?

That's the flip side of the coin, the ugly flip side of the coin. Black men who were husbands and fathers were stripped of their sense of manhood and power by not being able to affect or control the traumatic dynamics that took place against their household, against their woman, their wife, their daughters, and particularly their sons. There was no way to protect them, and if they tried in a very direct and aggressive way, they ran the risk of losing their lives, having their sons' lives taken and God-only-knows-what with the rest of their family. Black men had to learn to endure their aggression, their rage, their depression, their pain; they had to learn to internalize feelings.

So from the moment they arrived here, African-American men experienced a tremendous sense of powerlessness with no way to openly express what they were internalizing. When that happens, you have two choices. One is to find some kind of outlet, and generally what happens in that case is that you take it out on the people who are nearest to you. The other is that you shut down your emotions. That way you don't feel anything. I often think about Denzel Washington's character being tied to a post and whipped by the white officers commanding his black regiment in the Civil War movie *Glory*. He showed absolutely no expression. Black men have had to learn for centuries to endure, to deny that they are emotional beings, to cut off their expression of pain and rage. That, of course, does not allow them to be very comfortable with the tender side of their emotions. It especially makes it difficult to express those tender feelings to the woman you love, as well.

You mentioned that Denzel Washington showed no emotion. I certainly understand what you're saying, but my thought was that he was showing absolute, sheer, utter, ironclad defiance.

Yes. "I will not be broken; I will not be reduced to a crying, whining, two-year-old. I will stand here and be an ironclad man while I am experiencing all this incredible shame, incredible rage, incredible physical pain, but I will not allow any of you to know that."

I think that's been passed on among African-American men, like you pass on a banner, generation after generation after generation. That's where I believe the drugs and alcohol come in, because both are means of anesthetizing one's pain, one's rage, one's sadness, and one's shame.

Let me also say that femininity and masculinity issues in the black community are very sensitive issues. If you had several black men sitting in this room, they would say, "Look, I know who I am." It's a very sensitive issue that we used to throw under the rug, but now society is just beginning to talk about it. Michele Wallace was trying to start the discussion, I think, when she wrote the book *Black Macho and the Myth of Superwoman*. She was talking about why black men had to be so macho, why they have to oppress and depress black women. Some people say they need to try to gain some control and power in this society to feel like a man. Michele said she believed that most black males felt very emasculated, and were very angry about their lack of power. She believes this is why sexism exists so strongly in the black community. Many men say the "superwoman" strips them of their sense of masculinity.

If you're not being what you're supposed to be, and you're not fulfilling the role that you're supposed to have, certainly you're going to feel bad about yourself, but how do the people around you begin to feel about you?

The people around you, and specifically the women around you—your mother, your aunt, your sisters, your daughters, and your wife, or your lover—are going to have ambivalent feelings about you. They're going to feel on one hand, "You owe me. I've been carrying the weight of our culture and your confused sense of who you are for a long, long time. I've taken on what I felt you should have been about, plus I've carried out my own end of the bargain." And so they're going to feel frustrated, they're going to feel that it's important to try to get what's theirs. This is what I call the Entitlement Syndrome. They're going to feel ambivalent about wanting to be in a relationship with you, but also ambivalent about being without you. They're going to want what most women want, which is to be in partnership, to have a bond, to have companionship with someone, to raise a family, and that whole business. But why should I do that if I have to do it all on my own? If you're never going to be here? Or if you're going to be here but always giving me excuses, or if you're going to be here but not be able to carry your weight? Or if you're going to be here but not really connect with me emotionally? You're sitting here with me but there's no love connection. Many women say, "I feel so alone." So many women, particularly the married ones, say that they feel so lonely, so alone.

Could we suggest that maybe what's happening here is that the man builds an emotional facade around himself because the truth is too terrible? If we could make it safe for African-American men to say what their truth is . . .

If we could make it safe; that's a big if. I don't think black women can make it safe for black men. I think that if it's going to be safe, black men are going to have to make it safe for other black men. I have suggested for some time now a national "Black Male Movement" based upon affirming who they are emotionally. I think older black men must take the time to engage, model and support new thinking and gender training for younger men. Mini-groups need to form in churches, civic organizations, and college and university fraternities. Fathers, uncles and brothers need to reach out and confirm their brother, their fellow man.

But if it could be made safe, what do you think black men would say? What do you think they're really feeling behind the emotionless macho posturing?

I think they would say that it's exhausting; that it's tiring, that it's scary, that it takes so much energy to keep this ideal posturing out there to the world, that they feel threatened by the society, they feel the lack of having the means and the tools to fulfill the masculine role as it has been designed for men in this society. They would say they feel inadequate as men because they don't have the economic clout to do what they know they need to do for themselves, their families and their women. And that they feel terribly ashamed and vulnerable within a hostile society, and especially threatened by their women, who seem stronger than they are.

What are men afraid will happen to them if they express and expose and are honest about these insecurities that they feel?

That they'll be seen as whining. Terry McMillan, in her book *Waiting to Exhale,* called black men whiners. She said all they do is complain about what they don't have instead of making a way to get a piece of "the rock." Black men are concerned that what they're experiencing won't be understood or accepted as okay by others.

That's a reasonable apprehension on their part, isn't it?

Absolutely. It's absolutely reasonable. It's real. Some men have checked it out. Six or seven years ago I did a seminar in Ohio with black men and women. And at one point, we separated into male and female groups. I had a male partner and he took the men upstairs, and I went with the women. Both groups did some processing of what gender issues existed for them. Then the men decided they wanted to express to the women some things that they had never had a chance to say. So we came back together and had the men in an inner circle and the women around them in an outer circle, which was interesting in itself.

Who chose that configuration?

I don't remember. I just remember really struggling with that one, but if I had to do it over again, I would have put the women in the middle and the men on the outside, just in terms of what men are supposed to represent—the whole notion of protecting something that's "in." But it's interesting. The unconscious is very powerful. That's actually the way African-American relationships really look. The women are on the outside protecting, and the men are feeling on the inside.

So the men started expressing their pain and disappointment. They started expressing how they feel about not being accepted for who they are, for not having their struggle recognized, for having women respond to them in very self-centered ways where the women were only talking about what they needed, what they wanted. "You want, want, want all the time. Can't you see that I'm working with very limited resources? I'm doing the best I can." They were tired of the women complaining about them not expressing their feelings; they're expressing them to the best of their ability based on what they've ever seen as role models with their fathers and their grandfathers and their uncles, and why can't the women appreciate them for who they are, and for what they can do?

And as they were in the midst of talking about that, the women lit into them. I mean they fired at them! The women started screaming and yelling at them, "How dare they be so insensitive and uncaring!" and all the kinds of foul statements that can be made. And the men shut down. They shut down. They couldn't say another word. The male leader, at that point, described the dynamic. He said, "These men sat upstairs for an hour together, and struggled with their issues, got in touch with some feelings, felt supported by each other, and for the first time in their lives they had shared very intimate things with other men"—which by the way, many African-American men don't do; they do it on a one-on-one with a buddy, but not as a group; they'll talk sports and all the other stuff; I guess American men in general don't do it—"So it took a lot for them to do what they did. They wanted to share it with you. And you couldn't receive it as it was presented to you. You had to not only react to it, but then you had to tell them how they should see it, how they should feel about it, and label them, and say who they were, and why they were that way." So he had them look at this as typical of the kind of dynamic that goes on between a woman and a man.

Another little scenario you might find of interest happened in 1992 at a conference on the black family. We were first in a large, general session where people were talking about male-female relationship issues. Then we were to move into breakout rooms for smaller workshops. People had several workshops they could choose. So I was walking behind a group of men who were coming to my workshop. The women had moved to the breakout room immediately and gotten their chairs. When the men got to the door, they looked in the room, saw all these women sitting in there, and stopped. They didn't move. All of a sudden I hear one man say to the other, "I'm not going in there." So the other man said, "Doesn't look too good, does it?" The third man said, "Looks like a lynching to me." The fourth man said, "Yeah, and I've been hung too many times; I'm going downstairs." The black women were just sitting in there, just kind of chatting. They weren't being hostile. Nothing was happening yet. But already there was the anticipation of what was going to take place.

Where did their apprehension come from?

From their experiences in their communities, from watching black men and black women relate to each other. And from the knowledge that it seems so difficult to protect themselves with women. Men feel so threatened by women's power. Many men perceive women's power because black women seem to be able to do so much with so little. They more often are left in charge of everything. The male perception of women's power is so overwhelming that it creates power struggles between the sexes.

Let's assume that the women reading this book really do feel good will toward men. They want to help make things better. They are nodding their heads knowingly at your story of six or seven years ago in Ohio and they are willing to acknowledge that maybe they have some share of the responsibility in the problem . . .

Some, not all, but certainly some.

Yes. Some. What's the message that needs to be clear to the women who are nodding knowingly and saying, "Yeah, I've done that."

First, I want to say that many women really do want to know what they do to shut men off. Loads of them come to seminars, they come to counseling in much larger numbers than the men do, and they're always in search of self-help programs on TV, or textbooks or whatever. I think it's difficult to take a look at yourself and look at your part in the problems. They also want the men to work on themselves so they'll be better partners.

But I think sensitivity is the key. I'm seeing a large number of males now in my practice. They come in for individual counseling, which is refreshing. A lot of women say to me, "How do you get them to do that?" and "I don't believe they tell you anything in there!" And I say, "Oh, no, they do. They share very deep, personal secrets and experiences. They allow themselves to think about things that have brought them tremendous pain and shame and sadness. And they struggle hard to allow those feelings to be shown." I usually ask the men, "What allows you to do this here?" And the one thing they say is that they feel that I empathize, that I'm sensitive to what they've been through, that although I'm not male, I seem to be patient with their struggle, that I get to tap into some of these things that for generations have been turned off. When they come in my office, they get to experience me as a firm mother, direct mother, clear mother in terms of where they're going. I am confrontive. But I'm also caring, I'm sensitive, I'm open, I'm empathetic, and I give them a lot of nurturing feedback that says you are okay with me whether you cry, whether you scream, whether you slash out, whether you show me your humiliation, your pain, your sense of powerlessness, your joy, your clarity, all of that is okay. I accept all of it. Most people want acceptance if they're going to take risks and open up to another person.

Have you had men scream in your office?

Absolutely. Scream out at the anger, at their mothers, for holding them so close, so tight, so restricted, in a good way with good intentions to protect them, but feeling so stifled and overwhelmed by the rigidity of protection, that they make the association that to love a black woman is to lose all of your masculinity and power, personal power. And the other piece that they express around pain and anger is the lack of protection from their fathers in episodes with these women. The fathers would often go out the back door to get away from the woman who was screaming and yelling, so that they wouldn't have to endure. Or who would sit there in front of the TV or pull the newspaper up in front of them. Or go to bed. Or remember something that they needed to do with a friend or buddy, and go hang out with him until everything got calm in the house and the whole thing had blown over. Meanwhile, this young man would have to endure it by himself. This is so scary for a young boy, to deal with a woman's rage or control.

It sounds like the current situation is that we have women who, for a variety of reasons, are very strong, very powerful, very assertive, very much in charge.

At one level. But if you could hear a group of women talking about themselves and their relationships, you'd hear them feeling very tired and needy, you'd hear them talking about longing. Black women have always had the awesome burden of feeling responsible for the entire African-American culture, community, family, themselves, and their men. They feel so overwrought with the burden and so in pain about it, but at the same time, they feel enlightened that they have the ability to do it. It's a mixed bag, it's a bittersweet experience, because we know we can do it, but we also feel sad and weary and wish now that it could be shared. Black women want what most women want: compatible relationships with a significant other.

What do you think needs to happen to make things better?

We have lost, we are in the midst of losing, an entire generation of young black men, between the ages of fourteen and twenty-five, in the streets. We've got to begin to send the kids who will survive—and most of them will be women—a different message about loving, and about who they are, what their identities are, and how to relate to each other in very different ways, so that the black family will survive, so that the culture will survive. If you don't have stable family, you don't have culture. And if you don't have men, you don't have any of it.

Tell me what you mean by that. Are you talking about men in families here?

Yes. If you don't have enough men, how do you create two-parent households? And how do you create balance with a twosome arrangement? When there is only one parent, that one must try to do both the father's and mother's role. It's pretty difficult, and quite impossible for some to achieve. And the sons, I think, lose a significant developmental factor—male bonding for healthy gender identity.

There are those who would say that a family could be a mother with children, and you don't need a man to have a family.

Yes, a family can be a mother with children, but I don't think that black women can help black men to know who they are as men. The best mother in the world, with the best intentions and all of her time and energy and heartache, cannot do that.

One last thing I'd like to jump back to, just for a bit. You mentioned that the fellows in Ohio said what was on their minds, and the women shut them down. Did you pick up any body language or muttering from the men in the aftermath of having been shut down?

Yes. The men were disappointed. They were sad. When they left, they looked depressed to me, which meant that they were angry. But they didn't want to risk firing back at the women. They shut down and that was the end of it. They internalized their emotions, and looked the way Denzel Washington looked when he was being beaten.

The sad aspect of this is that both groups really wanted to understand what creates the tension between them. We must continue to find the answers together. We have come too far, for so many years in this struggle in America, to abandon each other now.

Jane Young

Since 1966, Jane Young has been a professor of English at a community college of the City University of New York, and since 1975, a free-lance writer. Her article "The Fathers Also Rise," an examination of the obstacles divorced fathers must overcome to remain significant figures in their children's lives, appeared in the November 18, 1985, issue of *New York Magazine*.

Jack: As you look at problems occurring today in New York City, do you see any connection between those problems and current attitudes toward maleness?

Jane: Sure I do. I see it at my school, an urban community college with more than fifteen thousand students, seventy percent of whom are female. The men in their late teens and early twenties are not going to college in the numbers they should be. A lot of the younger women already have children, and they have either never been married or were married and soon separated. Quite a few of them feel that it's okay never to be married at all, that marriage is probably not in the cards for them and that their kids will do just fine without fathers. Many of them didn't grow up with fathers themselves. The image that is held up is of the proud, strong, single heroine who struggles though her travails alone or with the help of other women—mother, grandmother, sisters, cousins, friends—and with her kids having little or no contact with their father. A lot of my women students really bridle when it's suggested that there is anything wrong with having a baby at fifteen or sixteen.

What effect do these dynamics have on the young men?

We know from psychological studies, which are widely ignored, that the cognitive development of young men without a father in their lives is considerably impaired, that fatherless young men are more erratic emotionally, that they often lack focus, discipline and motivation, that they're often not socialized and their ego strength is weakened. Their desire for masculinity expresses itself in extreme macho behavior. There is a kind of polarity in their lives. They are raised with and by strong women and they look for an equally strong image of masculinity, but it's not there. So they look out on the streets, but the authority figures in the community are too often criminals. And they posture, they are restless and aggressive, and they just roam. That's what the gang life is like. It's a substitute for family life in which maleness is valued.

Are you seeing these kinds of behaviors in your male students and their friends?

Yes, I see it in the behavior of males very often in the school environment. They are more likely to be late to class, absent, easily distracted, unable to concentrate, and more likely to give up and drop out when things get difficult. Young men are looking for something positive, and I think they are sad and forlorn, wishing to have a father. But they're not supposed to bring it up, because it might upset people and embarrass them. They are not supposed to miss having a father. But they do, both the boys and the girls. I think inwardly they do yearn.

Is it politically incorrect to say anything about the absence of a father, the deprivation of a father, that there might be at least a statistical possibility of an undesirable effect?

Totally. The accepted wisdom these days is that, as long as children are loved, it doesn't matter whether they grow up without a father or even a stepfather, and that fathers often do more harm than good. They are increasingly seen as verbally or sexually abusive, violent or physically and psychologically absent. Yet psychological studies consistently show that children in intact families generally do better than children growing up in single-parent families. No one wants to acknowledge the problem, because there are so many kids from divorced families and it's just too upsetting. There's a lot of denial about how much divorce messes kids up.

How do you think men are feeling these days?

I think men increasingly feel that women don't need them for the things they used to—as providers, protectors and heads of households—and, therefore, their status in relationships is limited. Media and government are telling women, "Get rid of this guy. You don't need him. You're probably better off on your own. We'll help you out so you can raise your children by yourself." So there is a tremendous sense of being rejected, scorned, vilified, and ultimately of not being important, except as a distant provider of money—and that creates a lot of rage. I also think that American men are very angry about what American women have accomplished in the past twenty years, educationally, economically, and socially. Yet no matter how strong a woman is, no matter how much of a feminist a woman is, she still tends to look down on men who are not sufficiently aggressive and successful. It's not enough for women to be achievers, to be, as Gloria Steinem once said, the men we wanted to marry. We still want men to achieve as much or more, and we have contempt for those who don't. They're marginal; they're losers.

Europeans have a saying that women are what they are, men are what they do. Is this what you are saying?

No, I am saying that women are what women are, and they increasingly do what men do, yet they want men to continue doing what men do. They haven't changed their expectations of men very much. Women feel very uncomfortable and threatened by the idea that men are not going to be strong, competent, substantial persons of status in the world. They're very suspicious of men who want, say, to be househusbands or who end up that way because they're unemployed or underemployed.

Are you detecting anything that tells you that men are not so interested anymore in doing what men are supposed to do?

I think there is more of a desire to be free to undertake the kind of self-development that women have often been able to explore because they were sheltered and protected by others. I think there is less of a desire to be a star or hit the top of the hierarchy by the time you are thirty. There is definitely a revolt against that.

So in a sense men are demanding what women have always had the option to be?

I just think men of all ages are increasingly resentful of the idea that they have to pour themselves into a career, climb the ladder, stay in lockstep. Lots of men in their thirties, forties, and fifties are divorced guys who are forced into a kind of bondage through divorce which forces them to go on making a living and producing economically at the same income level or better than they did before the divorce. I think men in those situations feel "I am stuck with this. I am glued into this thing and I don't want to be here anymore." A lot of them go into the underground economy to avoid being forced to pay support. They don't want to go on paying substantial sums of money to women they don't live with, for children they hardly ever get to see and who are taught that their fathers are no good even if they do see them.

One of the major differences between the resentment men feel toward women and the resentment women feel toward men is that one is expressed and one isn't. Does that seem accurate to you? Men's anger toward women isn't as expressed?

I think that women believe that men's rage at them is expressed in the doing; that is, men express their rage at women by verbally abusing them, by beating them up, by raping them or by leaving them and not paying child support. Often men punish women by withdrawing from them in a relationship. Men's hostile actions toward women are an expression of their rage.

Then might it be a good idea to legitimize men's verbal expression of rage?

Yes. Men don't openly say that they are angry at women, because it has become such an article of faith that they are not supposed to be mad at women. It's regressive.

Do you think women are interested in hearing from men how it is to be men?

No. I know I wasn't. When a man that I've known for a long time first came out of his unhappy, eighteen-year marriage, his wife and children came up to a suburban college where he was teaching. As he walked from the school to the train station they rode along beside him in their station wagon and his son threw his sneakers with a hole in them out the window. The boy yelled, "We can't even get any shoes because of you, because you left us." At the time and in the years since, this man kept playing this scene over and over in his mind. It was deeply painful to him that he was "abandoning" his wife and children, and that they were going to suffer. I didn't want to know about it. It was a male thing. And even to this day it is hard for me to empathize with his sense of his own responsibility for having hurt and "abandoned" these people. I also couldn't really identify with his pain at being separated from his kids, because women don't typically experience this after separation and divorce. I think my reactions are typical. There is a very great divide between men and women in this regard, I think.

Is it possible that one of the reasons a man might have trouble expressing powerful emotions is that he doesn't think he really has anything real or valuable or worthwhile to say, because men are dogs, men are pigs, men are scum?

There certainly is a devaluing of whatever it is men actually do feel and experience.

Yes. Do you think that's the answer?

It's bad. It has to be bad. Look what it results in. How can men's feelings be good and worthwhile if they always seem to end up hurting somebody?

Even before they hurt somebody. How can men's feelings be worth listening to if men are scum?

Not only are men scum but men are powerful, men run everything. If you have privileges, one of the privileges you don't have is for anybody to feel sorry for you. You can't be a victim. Also, if men say, "I am hurting," there is a lot of ambivalence about that, because the woman wonders, "Is this another way to get power over me?"

Might it be helpful in getting women to lower their suspicion and open their hearts for them to take an inventory from a man's point of view of how much power they have over men?

In the domestic sphere, anyway, women have power over men in a variety of ways. They can reject men, and because more and more of them earn some kind of living, they are increasingly ending relationships and marriages. They have tremendous power in the family because women spend a lot more time with children and have a lot more intimacy with them, and therefore influence. They are the mediators, the interpreters of the male presence in the home. If the mother says, "Daddy is a good person. We should honor Daddy, give him a Father's Day card, be considerate and respectful of him," then the children will have a generally positive image of their father. If she is always carping and complaining and criticizing Daddy in various subtle and not-so-subtle ways, the children are going to be more alienated from the father.

> A friend told me [that] at about thirty-five, he began to wonder who his father really was. He hadn't seen his father in about ten years. He flew out to Seattle, where his father was living, knocked on the door, and when his father opened the door, said, "I want you to understand one thing. I don't accept my mother's view of you any longer."
> "What happened?" I asked.
> "My father broke into tears, and said, 'Now I can die.' " Fathers wait. What else can they do?
>
> ROBERT BLY
> *Iron John*

That is a pretty significant power, isn't it?

Tremendous. The divorced father I mentioned earlier is an extraordinarily decent person in every way there is, kind and cooperative and supportive and in many ways an egalitarian, and he was married to a woman who had a very traditional notion of the roles. Mothering was something she was supposed to do, and he was just supposed to stay out of her way and supply the wherewithal to raise his "gifted children." And when his marriage ended, his estranged wife told his children that he wasn't a "real father" anymore, that he should be punished for leaving by being completely cut out of their lives, which is exactly what happened for ten years until his oldest child reconciled with him. All those years the children's mother told them their dad was not paying child support, when in fact he was paying over twenty thousand dollars a year. Children tend to believe what their mothers tell them. If mom says dad is a bastard, they tend to go along with her.

Instead of saying "traditional," could we say this woman had a very chauvinistic view of the roles?

You could call it that.

Could we say that she was trying to preserve female power for herself?

Yes, I would say that she was, and that society sanctions this sort of maternal power. I think the power trip for her was in being a breeder of prized children. She felt that she should be honored, revered and supported, and given a tremendous amount of control and authority because she produced gifted children.

She went to a sperm bank?

No. She did not go to a sperm bank, but she regarded the person who supplied the sperm as little more than that. I think women's power derives from the idea that women are naturally nurturing, that children will and should bond almost exclusively with the mother and that, even if the woman works and is away from the children for substantial periods, there should never be a situation where the mother loses legal custody of the child. The idea that the mother is the primary emotional caretaker of children gives her a tremendous amount of power, and a lot of women are clinging to that power. And a lot of that power is used routinely in ways that hurt men. We see it every day when men and women separate and children are involved. Women freeze men out, and it's very hurtful. There is no court on earth that can stop a woman from doing that if she has physical possession of the child.

Is there anything more we can say about women's power so that women understand how their power feels to men?

They have the power to shame men. The "all men are rapists" type of idea.

I felt very ashamed about the rape in New Bedford, Massachusetts, at Big Dan's Tavern. Do you know that case?

You mean the incident that was the subject the film *The Accused*, the gang rape in the bar?

Yes. Do you know the facts of that situation?

I have read about it and heard about it. I don't know what facts you mean.

Tell me what you believe to be the facts of that situation.

I have heard and read that a woman was gang-raped in a bar and that a lot of men looked on while this happened. In the film they were cheering, they were urging the other men on.

How many men were cheering in the film? I didn't see it.

I don't recall how many, but there were quite a few.

Is it your impression that this film is based on fact?

I had that impression. I had read about that case before.

What would you say if it turned out that there was no barroom full of cheering men?

Prosecutors have also substantially revised original reports that numerous bar patrons witnessed and even encouraged the rape with whoops and cheers. They say that aside from the six defendants and the victim, only three people were in the bar, and that the bartender and a customer sought to call the police, but were prevented from doing so by one of the six.

Time
March 5, 1984

Well, a rape is still a rape even if there is no mob of cheering men, but I would also say it indicates that Hollywood is ready and eager to buy into the feminist analysis that all men are predatory, and that it sells movies. God knows movies are filled with violent, predatory men.

Remember you talked to me over the phone a couple of years ago about a strong urge on the part of both feminist women and conservative women to get men out of the nursery?

Yes. Conservative women want hegemony over children because when women play that role, men have much less to do around the children and are therefore forced to go out into the world and behave like providers. The feminist woman sees the man's tender, sensitive, nurturing side as just a sneaky way to get more power over women after separation.

Is it possible that part of the vilification of men these days is an attempt to keep men out of the nursery? That that is precisely its purpose?

No developing society that needs men to leave home and do his [sic] "thing" for the society ever allows young men in to handle or touch their newborns. There's always a taboo against it. For they know somewhere that, if they did, the new fathers would become so "hooked" that they would never get out and do their "thing" properly.

Margaret Mead
Quoted by T. Berry Brazelton in
Maternal-Infant Bonding
Marshall H. Klaus, M.D., and
John H. Kennell, M.D.

Definitely. I think that has a lot to do with the feminist analysis of the nuclear family being basically a destructive force, not a positive one, and I think the idea is that if you keep men away from children, the male child will not be co-opted and inducted into the male culture.

Do you think that men have any reason to think that if they speak up, they are going to be mocked, as in "Oh, poor baby"?

I think it's worse than that. I think men are right to be afraid that if they stop playing the traditional economic role they have been assigned, women are going to get very uncomfortable, worried, angry and scared that this means he is going to cut out on her, or that he might want to do something that doesn't mean supporting her. He might get out of harness. And I think a lot of women would be upset by that. Women have a vested interest in men just doing what they do and doing it well.

What else would happen if men got out of harness?

Buildings wouldn't get built. Trains wouldn't run on time. Money wouldn't get made. I see these young guys, young profes-sionals, some of them are working seventy hours a week. They are highly paid slaves. Companies use them up.

Aren't they using up young women the same way?

No, not as much. Women have other outlets, other choices. They have other satisfactions in life.

Such as?

Babies. That is their out. Human things.

Rikki Klieman

RIKKI KLIEMAN is a trial lawyer in private practice, and an adjunct professor of law at Boston University. As a prosecutor in the 1970s, she handled cases of rape and other sex crimes. *Time* magazine named her one of the nation's top five female trial lawyers in 1983. She now defends clients against sex crime allegations, and in civil court she represents women who have sued men in sexual offense cases. She was born in 1948 and has been married since 1987. Her husband has three sons, in their early twenties, from a previous marriage.

Jack: *What do you see happening in the criminal justice system with allegations of rape?*

Rikki: There was a time when rape cases couldn't possibly be won by the prosecution, because the prosecution needed so much evidence of force and so much corroboration. Eventually the law changed to diminish this burden. Now, people can be charged with virtually no evidence. What's happened is that prosecutors are not exercising very much discretion in their choice of cases. In certain places in the country, I think they're exercising none. If a female comes in and says she was sexually assaulted, then on her word alone, with nothing else—and I mean nothing else, no investigation—the police will go right out and arrest someone. It seems to me that when that happens, the pendulum has swung too far.

I would be the first person to say that if someone sexually

assaulted a woman, then that person should be prosecuted to the fullest. However, I look at what's happening on college campuses in the sexual assault arena today, and I'm very frightened for young men. In the 1990s, a young man can be involved with a young woman in the slightest ambiguous act, and if she thinks about it the next day, two weeks later, five weeks later, whenever, and decides to say it was against her will, then that young man is in for some big trouble—a suspension, perhaps an expulsion and perhaps a criminal record. I think it's become outrageous.

What do you think is the motivation of the people who wish to scrutinize every ambiguous sexual encounter for criminal conduct?

I'm what I would call an "old feminist." I think that the "new feminists" do have some issues that are very important, but when I was a young woman in the sixties, when I started in the feminist movement, the idea was to "own" your personal identity as a woman. I do not think young women involved in new feminism are owning their personal identity. They're owning the collective identity and they see themselves as victims of men. Instead of being empowered, what they say is, "I as a woman should be able to go anywhere, do anything, at anytime and place I want and no one should bother me." Well, I think that's a rather naive way of looking at the world. Life is not so simple. So I say that women ought to be responsible for themselves. What young women are saying is that they have no responsibility and that men must have all responsibility, that they can come into any situation and the man must take one hundred percent responsibility to not do something that would offend them.

My thought is that both the man and the woman must each take one hundred percent responsibility, and both must control their own situation in a potential sexual encounter.

What are the issues facing a prosecutor who believes he or she might be dealing with a false allegation of rape?

First, let me say for the record, I defend the sexual offense cases that I choose to defend. I turn down eighty percent of the cases that come into my office. The ones I choose to take, I choose to take for a variety of reasons. In the sexual assault arena it is my personal viewpoint, not as a lawyer, but as a woman, that I will only take sexual assault cases where I feel that the person is not guilty, has been falsely accused. I don't like defending rapists. Now, to answer your question, when I prosecuted rape cases I would spend a long time dealing with the alleged victim. I worked for a superb district attorney who fully believed in the value of prosecutorial discretion. He was someone who would not prosecute every case that walked in the door. He believed in investigation. He believed in evaluation. He believed in judgments.

This is in Boston?

Just outside of Boston, in Norfolk County. His door was always open to discuss the appropriate use of discretion. And in the sexual assault arena, where I prosecuted a lot, I would talk with a woman who said she had been raped, and I think I was always very sympathetic. I was very compassionate. But I was also trying to unearth the truth. I went far out of my way with my police investigators, or with my victim/witness liaison people, to go back to the scene of the crime, to walk through it all, to see what else was out there, to talk to the accused person if he was willing to talk, to make an assessment about whether this was a truthful or false accusation. I think in many other prosecutors' offices, that does not happen. I think that too many prosecutors just take the word of the female— that's it—and don't investigate. I think if they did investigate, they would find false accusations.

I'll give you an example of a rape case I defended. A young man, a student at a college in Boston, goes out with a young woman, and eventually they go home together. He has roommates; they see this young man and young woman come in and go to his room. She brought her toothbrush, so she knew she was staying. Next day, she has breakfast with this young man and one of his roommates, and she goes off to school. About a week later he has not called her back. She asks him to a party. He doesn't want to see her again, for whatever reasons he has. He goes to the party with a different female, and the first young woman sees him there. Then she goes to a counselor at the university, and in her counseling session, talking about this young man, the conclusion is reached that he had sex with her against her will and that she was raped. The university police go and talk to this young man. He admits that he had sex with her. The next thing he knows, he is thrown in jail, a very bad jail. On her word alone. He has no idea what's happening.

Eventually I get the case. First of all, the university police knew nothing about any of the roommates having seen her the week before. They knew nothing about the toothbrush. They knew nothing about her having asked him to the party and his saying no. When I talked with young women in her dormitory, who knew her, she's described as being totally unstable. It wasn't like I had to do a lengthy investigation; they just handed this information to me. She's described as being a pathological liar by everyone, even her friends. In a system with a good prosecutor's office, when she first came to the police, an investigation should have followed.

Why did the investigation not follow?

I think it doesn't follow anymore because colleges and universities are afraid of being criticized. When they get a complaint like this, they just go for it. As I said, the pendulum has really swung. In many cases, young men are now the victims.

What would likely befall a prosecutor who dared to express any suspicion or actually inquired into and scrutinized an allegation of rape?

I think that's the fear: "What would happen?" I think that prosecutors have the visions of the horribles. They have visions, I suppose, of women's groups going to the press, of being personally attacked by women's groups. They would personally be held up to scorn and ridicule by the young woman and her parents. I think it's all a public relations issue; they're just terrified of being raked over the coals.

And the media would be willing collaborators, willing to lambaste the prosecutor as well?

I think the media handle news with whatever slant they choose to have. If some young woman or her support group go to the press and say, "Here is a young woman who was raped, and this prosecutor isn't prosecuting," I think they would develop a story. Then the prosecutor becomes the victim. The press is a very powerful factor.

[CBS News] correspondent Bernard Goldberg told me that "when it comes to gender issues, journalists generally have suspended all their usual skepticism. . . . We accept at face value whatever women's groups say. Why? Because women have sold themselves to us as an oppressed group and any oppressed group gets a free ride in the press. . . . I don't blame feminists for telling us half-truths and

sometimes even complete fabrications. I do blame my colleagues in
the press for forgetting their skepticism. . . ."

"Nobody in the media wants to look like a Neanderthal," Goldberg summarizes sarcastically, "so we just accept the feminist
agenda."

JACK KAMMER
The Quill
published by the Society of Professional
Journalists
May 1992

*In your experience, have prosecutors ever prosecuted a woman who
makes a clearly false, clearly malicious allegation of rape?*

I have never heard of them going back and prosecuting the
woman. That's a very interesting question, now that you bring it
up. Perjury prosecutions are rare, generally, but I have certainly
seen enough judges in nonsexual cases who, when they have seen
a primary government witness lie on the stand, when it is clear that
a witness is lying about a material fact, have sent perjury cases over
for prosecution. But I honestly don't know of that happening in a
sexual assault case.

*The defendants whom you believe to be falsely accused, how do they
feel?*

I've had two clients whom I believe were falsely accused who
committed suicide. One was accused of touching, molesting a child.
I think that kind of case is completely analogous to rape allegations,
because if a child says that a man molested him—or a woman
molested him, it could be either way—that case is going to get
prosecuted to the fullest, no matter what anybody thinks. When my
client left a suicide note and killed himself, I really considered
stopping my practice of law. To me it was an extraordinary look at
my own inability to help someone. I took it very much to heart,
because I thought one of my roles as a lawyer was to help people. I
think the publicity, the knowledge that his neighbors knew, the
knowledge that his colleagues knew—he was a professional man—
was too much. It was the end of a life.

The other one—which in certain ways was closer to me, because I had worked with this man a long time and I liked him so much—was a therapist. He was single and he met a woman at a party. They went off to a room upstairs at the party, they had sex, they came down, they talked to people at the party. About two, three weeks later, she called him; he didn't call her back. She went to the police, she said he raped her two or three weeks before. The police came to him. They asked him if he had been with her on this night, and he said yes. They asked him if he had sex. He said yes. They arrested him—again, on that basis alone—and charged him with rape. And when I say he was a therapist, the reason I think it's relevant is that he worked in family therapy, he worked with women, he really thought his professional life was over by the mere accusation, that no one would trust him anymore, that he could not be effective. I watched him deteriorate over a period of time. He couldn't cope. I've been greatly affected by those two events in my life. That's the worst that's happened.

What protects a man in this society with this criminal justice system from such a violation?

Not much. There is only one way to fight it, or to regain your dignity, and that is with the use of a good lawyer. It's not always justice just for the rich, but good lawyers can be expensive.

Have you ever heard from ideological feminists that when a woman says she's been raped, she's been raped?

Yes. As you can tell by now, I think that is absurd.

What motivates such a statement?

I have good friends, women friends, who get upset with me when I become angry with that statement. They say, "If a woman says she's been raped, she's been raped. Why would you believe the man?" And these are very intelligent women, these are professional women, these are women who have been around. And I say, "Why wouldn't you believe the man if he says he didn't rape her? Why should one be believed rather than the other?"

What's the answer to that question? Why should the woman be believed and the man disbelieved?

Because it's the feminist point of view that a woman would never say she was raped unless, of course, she was raped, because why in heaven's name would any woman ever say that if it were not true?

What do you think of the consensual sex contracts that some men's groups have been circulating?

> Neither of us may claim to be the victim of sexual harassment or assault or rape as a result of the acts which are the subject of this agreement. By signing this contract we acknowledge that the anticipated sexual experience will be of mutual consent. . . .
>
> We understand that no provision of this agreement relieves us of the obligation to treat each other with caring and mutual respect. . . .
>
> excerpts from "Consensual Sex Contract"
> National Center for Men
> Brooklyn, New York

When I started to speak on this topic, I was called to some fraternities, and I said that one of the answers to this whole dilemma is education and communication. I said, "Maybe what you need is a written contract." I said it as a joke. But it's not such a joke. How do you protect yourself from being falsely accused? I don't know. Maybe that's the way. It certainly takes a lot of the romance out of sex, I would think.

Do we have any idea what percentage of rape allegations are clearly false?

I have no idea. And I say to you that anyone who tells you they have an idea is wrong. If there's no recantation, who is to say it's false for statistical purposes? Now, I know that everybody comes up with statistics. I'm sure the new feminists would say it's a minuscule percentage, and on the other hand I know there is a study in the Air Force, where the statistic of false accusations is enormously high—over fifty percent. And there are FBI statistics, there are police statistics, and I say none of them are valid. None. My guess, though, is that there are many false accusations, but I don't know how to give you a statistic on it.

Let's talk for a minute about the other side of this problem. It's pretty clear how false accusations of rape hurt men. How do false accusations of rape hurt women?

I think they hurt women in a number of ways. False allegations play right into that bad, old stereotype of the screaming, shrieking "woman scorned" that "hell hath no fury like." The next woman who really has been assaulted, really has been raped, might not be believed because of the false accusation of the previous woman.

You've been outspoken on your views of false accusations of rape. What reaction do you get from the public?

I've gotten only three or four letters against my position. They've been wicked letters, but what's interesting is that I've received many letters—I'd say probably twenty to thirty letters—from women, and some from men, who support my position.

What are the women expressing to you about their support for you? Why do they want you to be doing this?

I think there are a significant number of women who feel that the new feminist movement is not the voice of reason on this subject. I see myself as someone who's building bridges between women and men, among women and men. I think that there are many women out there who would like to see this issue discussed in a world of reason, not of emotion.

You mentioned that some of the letters were from men. Was there anything generally different in the letters from men?

The men would give a personal thank-you. They appreciated that there was a woman who saw that there could be a reasonable point of view, that there were two sides to this story, or more than two sides, actually.

And the women who wrote these letters to you—are they concerned about their sons, their brothers, their uncles, their husbands?

I've had a couple of those. I've had more of that in conversation, much more. It's an interesting point. The new feminists will see one day, if they have sons, how they feel about some of these issues.

Do you see men doing much to protect themselves against false accusations of rape?

Not enough. I think that there's more activity now going on in the colleges and universities, which I'm very glad to see. There are fraternity groups, there are men's groups, there are support groups, there are educational groups that are forming. They begin with a dialogue among the men, and then some create a dialogue among men and women together. I think that's excellent. I think college-age men are becoming aware. I don't know about groups in society outside of college-age groups.

Are these groups in which men get together and say "Hey, we need to protect ourselves against false allegations of rape," or is it men getting together and saying "We need to confront and take responsibility for the bad things that we do to women"?

I think it's probably both and more. A great number of men have consciousness-raising groups which are in your latter category. They're blaming themselves about the bad things some men do to women. It might be productive, but I think that it's not so much that young men are doing bad things to women as it is that they are doing ambiguous things. It's that people don't know how to communicate. It's that people don't know the limits of their sexuality. They don't know what the other person means, what the woman means with her body language, what she means with her spoken language. I don't think it necessarily has to go to the extreme of "How do I protect myself from a false accusation?" I think the question has to be, "How shall we conduct ourselves as men? What are our standards? How should we communicate with women?"

And on the other side, is there any effort on the part of women to get together and discuss how they should conduct themselves with men?

Yes. I think there is. My question is, of course, who's leading these groups? I think there are many women's groups all around the country. In the colleges and universities they're everywhere. But my fear is that they may lapse into "what men have done to us" groups, "we are victim" groups, instead of being women's groups that are talking about being able to set standards with a willingness to communicate. If I had a capsule goal here, it would be for women and men to become educated and communicate with each other to create an environment that's safe, that has attainable standards of behavior for both sexes, so that people can relate with integrity.

Carolyn Baker

CAROLYN BAKER, Ph.D., is a consultant in human and
organizational development and, since 1980, has worked with individuals and groups on issues of recovery, surviving dysfunctional families, and gender. Carolyn lives in Santa Rosa, California. She was
born in 1945 and is single.

Jack: *You've been drawn to the men's movement for the past three
years or so. What about the men's movement attracted you?*

Carolyn: I had been working on my personal issues about my
father. I grew up as an only child in a Fundamentalist Christian
home in the Bible Belt of the Midwest with a "rage-aholic" mother.
A rage-aholic is a person who uses rage as a defense mechanism to
cover or avoid fear or grief, and actually becomes addicted to raging. My father was a businessman, but very passive, very unin-
volved, very wimpy. I always knew that my father loved me, but he
never really took part. He brought home the paycheck, did all of
those things that men are supposed to do, but did not father. Then
there was a conference in June of 1991 in San Francisco called
Tough Guys, Wounded Hearts. It was a three-day conference, but
I was only able to attend one day. Do you want to hear all this?

Yes, please.

I had never been to an event like this. I felt so extraordinarily
supported. I had been involved in the women's movement for

twenty or twenty-five years and had never been to this kind of mixed gathering. Whenever I was at a gathering that had to do with gender, it was for women only, and the men would have been trashed if they had tried to get in. So here are these men opening up to us. Men would greet me and say, "You are such a beautiful woman, I am so glad you're here today." I thought, "Holy mackerel, what's going on here?" At the closing ceremony, one of the facilitators said, "Let's have the women in the center." So there were three hundred men making a circle around us as they sang an African tribal song, a salute to the goddess, a tribute to the feminine. I had never been in a room with men drumming, but here were three hundred men, maybe seventy-five women, and all this power and energy coming from these men. And so then I'm really in tears, I couldn't hold it back anymore.

Do you know what it was that was reaching you?

I didn't at the time. What I know now is that it was stirring up stuff around my father. I had just never felt really connected with males, not in a heart way, and here it was, it was possible, it was what I had always wanted.

You see, I was raised in some ways very much like a man. I had to be strong and tough and stifle my feelings and essentially take care of my mother. There was a lot of emotional incest as well as physical abuse and sometimes I felt more like her husband than my father did. So, I feel tremendous resonance with some of the issues that men are struggling with.

I want to share with you a poem I wrote recently to express how I identify with men and the internal work they're doing. It's very autobiographical.

It's called "Family Reunion."* I'll just read parts of it.

Where are you my beloved brother
With the drum in your hand
Dancing around the fire of the sacred Masculine
All hairy and sweaty and delirious with delight
*   in newly-discovered embodiment?*
Your drumbeat pierces my heart, and my chest

---

* "Family Reunion" © 1991 Carolyn Baker

*Begins heaving with sobs because I feel your pain and
your joy.*

*Did you say you're grieving the loss of your father?
So am I.*

*Did you say he was like some faded necktie hanging
silently in a dark hallway closet where the door is
only opened when company comes?*

*Did you say you felt suffocated by your mother's loneli-
ness and sometimes felt more like her husband than
your father did?
So did I.*

*Oh, my brother, it seems that we grew up in the same
family but never saw each other until now.*

*That's beautiful. Thank you. I love the reference to your father as
being a what? A limp necktie?*

A faded necktie hanging silently in the hallway closet. A ghost.

*You mentioned that your father was wimpy. What was happening at
the times his wimpiness was most apparent and most painful to you?*

I remember my father as either sitting and reading the Bible or
sitting and doing his bookkeeping, working on his business.

*Were there ever times when you wanted him to apply his strength to
your situation when he didn't do so?*

One time when I was a senior in high school my mother was
really on the rampage. She knew that I was going to be leaving
home and going to college, and of course she couldn't talk about
that or deal with that consciously. She was in a rage and just crazed,
raging and angry at everything. I was fighting with her a lot. She
got pretty abusive, very verbally abusive. I remember one evening
in the summer she was throwing and breaking things and I had just
about had it with her. I didn't have the words for it, but if I had,
I probably would have said, "Somebody get me out of here. Somebody help me." Then she took off in a rage and went out driving
somewhere. I was relieved when she left, and my dad, of course,
had been in his little office doing his stuff.

Did he know what was going on?

He heard it, and when he heard the breaking and the throwing and her slamming the door and leaving, he got up and came out. And just kind of stood there. I'll never forget; he just stood there helplessly as if to say, "Well, I don't know what to do." Then he just stammered, "Well, do you want to go get some ice cream?" And I said "Yeah." So we went to get some ice cream, and I don't think we talked five words the whole way. He just couldn't talk. It took that much of an uproar for him to come out of his room and be with me, and even then he was just barely there.

When your mother was raging, and your father was in his little room, and you wanted him to come out, what did you want him to do? What could he have done? He opens the door while she's raging and what does he do?

Stop her, tell her to stop raging. If she won't stop raging, then physically contain her somehow without hurting her and take me out of there, and just say "I love you. I'm not going to let you be treated this way. I'm your dad, I'm going to protect you. We're outta here."

I can understand why you referred to your father as wimpy. When you were at the gathering of three hundred men who were drumming, and feeling like you were finally getting the connection with men you never got from your father, what adjective would you apply to them?

Two words. Gentle strength. That's what I wanted from my dad.

The popular image, the media image, of the men at the conference you found so powerful is that they are like faded neckties.

You think so?

Wimpy. I think the popular image is that they're wimpy. The average man and woman in the street, I think, believe these guys are there just to cry and hug trees. What would you want them to understand?

When you walk into a room of all of these men drumming, and you feel this powerful masculine energy that is there to protect and serve humanity, the earth, women, children, other men, all of life, there is nothing wimpy about that.

What would you say to people who just cannot juxtapose the concepts of masculinity and serving life?

I guess I would say that they don't really understand what masculinity is. For me that's an inherent part of the masculine: serving life.

Could you serve up for me just a little bit of the rhetoric out there that denies that fact about masculinity?

You mean things like men are patriarchal and self-centered, don't give a hoot about the earth, and they're greedy, polluting— that kind of stuff?

Yes. Could you go on for a little bit with that?

They're just interested in working and fucking and possessing, acquiring, raping the earth. What else?

Causing war.

Oh, yeah. War-mongering, posturing, territorial.

That's good. I mean, it's bad, but thank you. What is your current relationship with your father?

Shortly before the Tough Guys conference, I could no longer continue to just have a relationship with my parents where my abuse was not addressed. Many people discover when they are working with abuse issues that they can't stay in denial with their families anymore; something has to be said. So I decided to confront my mother. I wrote her a long letter. At the same time I wrote my father a long letter, and included a copy of my letter to her with my letter to him. This was June of '89. I got no response, nothing, from either of them. Two years went by. In May of '91 I heard from my cousin that my father had been in a car accident. I didn't know how badly he was hurt.

So I called up to talk to him and my mother answered the phone. I said, "I want to talk to my dad," and she reluctantly gave him the phone. We started to connect. "Hi, how are you?" back and forth. Then I said, "What happened to you?" and he began to tell me, but then he went right into "I wish you could talk to your mother." Once again, he can't deal with me, he's pulled away from me. There's always been this triangulation in the family. He could never just—he never felt free to really have a relationship with me. So right away he said, "I wish you could talk to your mother, I wish you would apologize." I said, "There's nothing to apologize for." Well, she got on the extension and started screaming at him, "Hang up, hang up, don't talk to her! Hang up, hang up!" I realized the best thing I could do was hang up and so I hung up. On my birthday that year, three months later, I sat down and I wrote him a letter and I put in that letter everything I would ever want to say to my father. I poured out my heart—I still have the letter—my love for him as well as the truth, as I saw it, of our family. The letter came back three times refused with her handwriting on the envelope. Finally, I sent it certified to him, got it back "refused" with *his* handwriting on it. A couple of weeks later I got a letter from my father telling me that he could no longer consider me his daughter. And I'm still grieving that one.

Did he say why?

Because of the "lies" that I said about my mother, and until I apologized to her he doesn't want any contact with me. That's how tied up by her he is. That's how much he's allowed himself to be tied up by her.

I was going to ask what your primary feeling was toward your father. What would you say it is?

I would have to say both love and anger. And I feel that it's really unfortunate that my father can't know me, because I'm a good woman, I'm a good person. He should be able to know me.

And he doesn't know that about you. Do you know that he's a good man?

Yes.

How do you know that?

Because he gave me a lot of good stuff. I watched him over the years. There are a lot of qualities in my father that I really respect. He's a man of integrity in a lot of ways. I don't think he ever screwed anyone in business. I think he got screwed because he didn't sometimes. He's an articulate man. He's got a good mind. He writes well. He's got a good heart.

What I would like to do now would be to see if there might be any connections between your situation with your father and the broader situation of women and men. Do you see any parallel?

Well, it's interesting. I'm involved with a gender healing group in Sonoma County. There are about thirty of us, men and women, *who come together once a month. Most of us are healers or in the helping professions. About two months ago we had a meeting where the women talked about our father wounds, and the men listened. The men were just blown out of the water, because what we said was so similar to their experience. They had the same experience of loss, the same resultant mistrust of men and masculinity, either because of the father's lack of presence, or because of the father's power and control and abuse—the opposite of lack of presence. My experience is that we are all—men and women—profoundly affected by our experience of father.*

Either way, whether it's too wimpy or too controlling, the problem is the absence of healthy masculinity. That's why it was good to hear you connecting masculinity with positive things, serving life. The concept of healthy masculinity doesn't get a lot of discussion in America today.

Right.

Another concept that doesn't get discussed much is the concept of unhealthy femininity. What do you think needs to be said about that?

One of the reasons that I appreciate archetypal psychology so much is the distinction that Jung makes between the masculine and feminine functions on the one hand, and patriarchy on the other. We tend to confuse the terms "patriarchal" and "masculine," as if they're synonymous. Certainly the feminists tend to make those synonymous. As I said in "Confessions of a Recovering Feminist,"* that article you first saw of mine, I believe that patriarchy is a way of life based on power and control and exploitation. I see it as the marriage of the dark feminine and the negative masculine. If we're going to understand and dismantle patriarchy, we need to be talking about the dark side of the feminine, as well as the negative masculine.

What needs to be said?

What needs to be said is that we women need to look at the feminine shadow so that we can stop competing for the victim role. We need to get off it and, yes, own that we have been victimized, but also own that men have, too. We don't have a corner on the victim role. There is plenty of victimhood to go around and we have to start looking at our feminine shadow and own that as a part

* Reprints available at no charge from Carolyn Baker. Send SASE to 1901 Cleveland Avenue #2; Santa Rosa, CA 95401.

of ourselves and stop projecting it onto males and onto the masculine.

Tell me how that projection is working.

It creates the idea that only men abuse. It's only men who are patriarchal. It's only men who are controlling, or greedy, or competitive, all of those things you asked me a while ago about the synonyms that get attached to men and masculinity. Women are capable of just as much viciousness, cruelty and abuse as men.

What is going on in America in the 1990s that makes it so unusual to acknowledge these truths?

Well, I think it's changing. I really do. We've just come out of recognizing thousands of years of oppression of women and we're in a real transition from looking at that oppression, owning that oppression, making tremendous social changes to try to rectify that oppression and now realizing that we have to go further, that that's not enough, that we can't stay in that victim role. My perception is that feminists are really hanging on to "we've been victimized, we've been victimized, we've been victimized," and are not yet at the place of looking at the feminine shadow. Women need to get beyond the purely political and sociological aspects of the women's movement and become more deeply grounded in feminine spirituality, to look at their own darkness. When we keep it up here with the political only, then we're in our heads, we're not in our bodies. We have to look at our wholeness and our humanness; part of our wholeness is our darkness. Women who stay in the political and in the mental aspect of these issues end up doing the same thing they're accusing of men of doing, being in their heads and away from their hearts.

If we could bring it up into the light and talk more honestly about the fact that women, like men, are capable of doing bad things to the other gender, what would happen?

We would take a big step toward healing. My experience in gatherings of men and women is that they start with men on one side of the room saying "You, you, you, you, you . . ." and women on the other side saying "You, you, you, you, you . . ." But if we keep talking, keep hearing each other's pain, keep hearing each other's anger, the results can be phenomenal. It can change everything.

Carol Iannone

CAROL IANNONE, Ph.D., is a professor of literature and writing at New York University's Gallatin Division. She is a vice-president of the National Association of Scholars (NAS), an organization formed to combat the politicization of higher education, a phenomenon now commonly known as political correctness. She is a consulting editor of *Academic Questions*, the journal of NAS, and has written for *Commentary* and other periodicals.

Jack: *You were once a feminist. What caused your disenchantment with feminism?*

Carol: I taught feminism and literature as a teaching assistant at the university level. I started being skeptical after being interviewed for a teaching job by a couple of feminists. Then I did my dissertation on feminism, and through the process of doing my dissertation, I came to feel that feminism was really a very limited, and in many instances, totally false, ideology.

Can you tell me about the interview that made you skeptical?

In the mid-1970s, I interviewed at a university in upstate New York for a job teaching three courses, only one of which was concerned with feminism. Before being interviewed by the chairman of the department, I was interviewed by the department's two very radical feminists. They picked me up at the train station and took

me to a Howard Johnson's to talk. Since only one of the courses was
going to be on feminism, why send two feminists to interview me,
outside the school, by themselves? These two women were very,
very harsh on me, especially one of them, and I could feel that
there was no way to please them except by being a radical, committed, ideological feminist.

At that time I had the liberal idea that there was a liberal way to
be a feminist. You didn't have to be radical; you didn't have to be
a zealot; you could have a general feminist outlook and you could
look at literature in a generous way, using some feminist ideas: what
were the women characters doing? What was the importance of
women? What was the writer's view of women? But it seemed to me
that these two women wanted strong ideological statements against
certain writers, and claims that other writers were strong supporters
of feminism. They wanted to use literature to show women "what
the culture thinks of them." They wanted to know quite specifically
how my course was going to be feminist, and how my dissertation
was going to be feminist. They wanted to know what conclusions I
had reached. They were not interested in my dissertation as a mode
of inquiry.

This was or was not the official job interview?

This is the thing. After they raked me over the coals, and made
it very hard for me, they brought me back to be interviewed by the
chairman, but it seemed that they pretty much had the final say,
that they signaled to the chairman, "She's not for us." After that,
the interview with the chairman was a mere formality. He had very
much allowed them to have the say, because they were rabid ideologues.

What was going on with the chairman?

I think he was cowed; he was one of the old school. That's one
of the things that has happened in the academy. Academics were
generally too liberal to oppose what was coming. It's how radical-
ization happens; liberalism is often not strong enough to resist it.

I was staggered; I was dazed. Feminism was supposed to be a
movement full of people who were going to create a new kind of
world, to get away from all the things that men have done wrong,
all the kinds of backbiting, and jealousy, and invidiousness, and

power plays. I don't know what I thought it was supposed to be. My hope for feminism was silly, liberal, utopian nonsense. I really thought this movement was something new in the world; I really did. I even remember describing to a friend how everything we think is coming out of the "male grid." Everything. Therefore, there's an entirely new way we can begin to think and conceptualize when we get rid of that male grid and work in a female mode. I really thought it could change the world. And after dealing with these two radical feminists I was utterly staggered.

My adviser, a woman, said, "This is going to happen in any movement; this is not what feminism is in general." But I did not buy that. I felt I had seen something. It reminded me of the Russian Revolution. People supported it through all the purges and the terror. Even revolutionaries about to be executed by their own revolutionary regime could not let it enter their minds that the revolution was actually corrupt. It was about power; it wasn't a genuine revolution about the working man. This was that kind of experience for me.

Then I took an adjunct job at a college in New Jersey, and one of the courses that I was given to teach was Women's Lives. It was really just a consciousness-raising rap session. I took it over from somebody else in the middle of the semester, so a whole dynamic was already set up among the women in the class.

One of the other students said to me privately, "I don't know if you've picked it up, but there's a real intimidation in that class. Those two control it; a lot of us are afraid to say what we want to say." So I, stupid liberal once again, in the next class say, "It's come to my attention that some of you feel a little intimidated; I don't want you to feel that. I want you to feel open." The two demanded, "Who said that?" So I said, "I don't think I have to tell you, but there is a feeling that we need to be a little more free and easy and tolerant." "Who said it?" There was a real confrontation. I didn't want to reveal the person and put her on the spot. And they said, "This is a class with a personal dimension and we have to be honest and free, and know who's saying what." When I refused, they stormed out of the class, and went to the head of women's studies; they reported me.

For what violation? They couldn't have called it sexual harassment, could they?

No, not in those days. The grievance was something impossibly vague—mishandling a class, perhaps. At any rate, they withdrew from the class and got an agreement that someone else would read their papers; the school went along with that.

Another example of lack of courage on the part of the administration?

I think so. The head of women's studies called them ideologues. I said, "I'm sorry, but when that kind of thing happens, it makes me very discouraged about feminism." And she said to me, "They control the Women's Center and they're very forceful, they're very energetic, they tend to get power." It sounded like she was all for me, but I was never invited to teach in that department again. This is how radical movements work. The people in them have much more energy, they're feeding on an ideology much more than any liberal ever could. The liberal doesn't have a chance against it. The liberals just say, "Oh, well, those are just the extremes."

> Male faculty members at Baylor University . . . are hiring lawyers . . . because a female colleague . . . filed a complaint with the Equal Employment Opportunity Commission in November 1992 after taking the matter up with the university's Sexual Harassment Mediation Board, the Fort Worth Star Telegram said. . . .
>
> In response, Baylor administrators asked [three tenured professors] to accept early retirement. . . .
>
> "There's not any law that says you've got to like the guy or gal working next to you," said [one defendant's attorney]. . . . [D]isliking someone is a far cry from sexual harassment."
>
> It is not clear what started the squabble.
>
> One version . . . bases the rift on a faculty meeting at which a man lambasted a feminist journal.
>
> UNITED PRESS INTERNATIONAL
> April 10, 1993

Why are the liberals so weak?

They're too polite. They think everyone's playing the gentleman's game, the way they are. They don't see that some people are really out for power and are not playing a gentleman's game. Some people don't want both sides; they want control. The liberal often does not have a sufficient grasp of what you have to do with radical evil. He thinks you can always talk it out. You can always reason it out. He doesn't know that you're often dealing with something that's irrational.

Where are the conservatives?

We founded the NAS, the National Association of Scholars, to fight the politicization of the academy, better known as political correctness. We've had conferences; we have a journal; there have been books. We try to highlight what's going on. It appears, though, that the dominance of the illiberals is getting worse.

Speaking of political correctness, what do you think of Donna Shalala?

Bad news, very bad news. She epitomizes political correctness with her efforts to bring a speech code to the University of Wisconsin. But it's interesting. She wasn't appointed to be secretary of education.

I'd feel much more comfortable with her as secretary of education. In Health and Human Services, she has dominion over welfare, child support and family issues.

Yes. She could further the whole breakdown of the family, setting up women in a life independent from men, but using the government as a support.

Socialized fatherhood.

Yes. Socialized, anonymous fatherhood. That's right. Clinton emphasized welfare reform in his campaign, but he chose someone who holds that as a very minor priority. There you have it.

Back in your feminist days, what did you find compelling in feminist ideology?

I imagine it was similar to the experience of people first reading Marx and feeling that the whole world just fell into place. Feminism explains everything; it's a totalistic ideology. It gave a clearly identifiable reason for the misery of human life: the imbalance between the sexes, male power gone amok. You could explain everything that way. Religion could be explained that way. Many pieces of literature could be explained that way. The sense of inadequacy that many young women feel seems to be explainable by feminism. It's exciting to have something that explains the whole world to you. There's a promise of salvation in feminism. "If we do it right, if we correct this imbalance, we create a new world." It's a way of looking at life that permits all evil to be ascribed to a discrete cause. If that discrete cause were addressed, all evil would be eliminated.

And this discrete cause is . . . ?

Men. Patriarchy. Sometimes it's men, specifically men, individual men, Everyman; sometimes it's men in general, or the male mindset, male attitudes, patriarchy in an abstract sense apart from what individual men do. It has different manifestations. Different people will put it in different ways.

And in the utopian view, what would be done with or to men?

I suppose that here again you'd probably have variety, but I think generally men would be reeducated to express themselves differently, to eliminate from their activity, and even from their thought, the modes and attitudes that create difficulties in human existence. Patriarchy would be dismantled, all the structures by which men have power over women, even without personally asserting it, would be dismantled.

You used the word "reeducated." That's a scary word.

Yes. And in fact in those days, in the very beginning, no one could have thought that it would be so specifically applied, but now we actually have the sensitivity workshops, the date rape workshops, the sexual harassment workshops. We're actually trying to reeducate the mind and hearts of individuals to this new ideology.

Let's talk about the article you wrote about the case of Sears Roebuck versus the EEOC, the Equal Employment Opportunity Commission. The situation was that Sears was one of the most progressive corporations in trying to promote women through its ranks. Sears was making a good-faith effort to bring women into the corporation, give them good opportunities. Who was it who first alleged discrimination?

It was the EEOC itself. Even though they compiled evidence for eleven years, they never found a single woman willing to say that she felt personally discriminated against.

So in the absence of seeing any real victims . . .

They used the statistics.

They simply looked at the numbers.

Right.

And the numbers were clear that women were earning less money . . .

The big money is in commission sales. Very few women were in commission sales, selling the heavy-duty stuff: tires, furnaces, aluminum siding. You sell the heavy-duty stuff and you can make big money, but it's almost all commission. You don't have much of a salary. Plus, it's weekend work, it's night work; you go to people's homes, you work on a prospective sale for a period of time. That's where the money is. The noncommission sales are in the stores, selling bedding and pillows and things like that. You have a regular salary, regular hours, but you don't have an opportunity to make big money. And the EEOC found very few women in commission sales. They said this must be discrimination; women are not being allowed to take this better kind of work.

[A spokeswoman for the California] pay equity committee said anecdotal evidence indicates that the sales jobs men get are considerably different than slots for women.

"Men tend to sell larger things such as cars and boats, and women tend to sell clothing or cosmetics," she said. "Those higher-ticket items get higher commissions." . . .

"Among full-time workers, men on average work more hours than women," [a Stanford professor of labor economics] said.

DENNIS J. OPATRNY
San Francisco Examiner
March 28, 1993
in a page one story headlined: "Men Make a Buck, Women Earn 60¢"

It's the patriarchy; it's men being threatened by women's success; it's male chauvinism; it's discrimination; it's an injustice to women.

Right.

It's the Glass Ceiling.

Right. Women are not being given these promotions, because somebody thinks they can't do it or shouldn't do it.

The idea that Sears was bad here is an idea that doesn't just reflect the EEOC's idea of Sears, but our society's understanding of our whole economy. If women aren't making big bucks, it's because of discrimination.

If women really earned 59 cents to the dollar for the same work as men, what business could compete effectively by hiring men at any level?

WARREN FARRELL, Ph.D.
author of *The Myth of Male Power: Why Men Are the Disposable Sex*
writing in *Network*, the newsletter of the National Congress for Men and Children
Spring 1988

Absolutely. If it isn't fifty-fifty, it must be discrimination.

When the average woman hears this kind of thinking, what's her reaction?

I'm sorry to say that I don't agree with some conservatives who say that the average woman has no truck with feminism. I think she has a lot of truck with feminism. She has enjoyed some of the things feminism has given her. It's given her a lot of ways of looking at her life. And a lot of excuses. I think that very often women do feel that they've been discriminated against. That's what's so terrible. The picture starts growing and growing and women start to believe that there really is this mass conspiracy to keep them in place just because the numbers aren't there.

So the idea that there is a Glass Ceiling, the idea that women are being discriminated against, in jobs and businesses, is causing women to be angry, unhappy, upset at men?

Yes, that they've not been given a fair shake in life.

Despite the best efforts of the EEOC to demonstrate discrimination, Sears demonstrated that there are other causes for what we popularly perceive to be a Glass Ceiling.

Yes.

What are the other causes?

A researcher, a feminist, named Rosalind Rosenberg, using the research that she and other feminists had developed, testified truth-fully that women do traditionally take jobs that coordinate with family life, they do tend to like jobs where there is a regular salary and regular hours, they don't particularly like weekend and night work, they don't like the insecurity of commission sales where they don't know what they're going to be earning from week to week, they want a certain kind of flexibility on the job rather than having to give themselves over to it. All these things operated on women not wanting to go into commission sales. Some of that information came from the work of another feminist researcher who testified for the EEOC against her own research. She got on the stand and contradicted what she herself had written about women in her own work.

Was the EEOC believing that every woman was out there one hun-dred percent, working to try to make money?

Yes. Or at least that was the tack they took.

At the time you wrote your article, in 1987, the EEOC was going to appeal. Has the appeal been heard?

Yes. Sears won.

Did the EEOC finally give up?

They gave up; that was it.

:   [U.S. District Court] Judge Marilyn Hall Patel . . . ruled in Au-
:   gust that the [Lucky Stores supermarket] chain was guilty of system-

: atic discrimination towards women in its hiring and promotion
: practices. . . .
:   The ruling left the chain open to tens of millions of dollars in
: back pay for 20,000 former and current employees. . . .
:   Lucky filed a mid-trial petition to . . . have the judge removed
: from the case, claiming she had . . . "made statements that intimate
: she's not listening to Lucky's arguments."
:
:
:   United Press International
:   April 9, 1993

What happened to Rosalind Rosenberg?

She's been vilified by the feminist academic community, and
apparently booed at conferences; she had to take a lot of heat for
telling the truth. But she was tenured, so she's okay.

*Could you describe what you've written about the bald statements
some feminist scholars have made about the proper use of feminist scholarship?*

You have to say that there are some legitimate areas of inquiry.
You could legitimately look into specific areas of women's history,
for example, women in the labor force. But you can't control the
outcome. If the outcome says that women have different ways of
responding to opportunities to earn money, then you have to admit
that. What feminist scholars do is dishonest. The scholar is supposed to find the truth and present it, regardless of how it's used.

Are we saying that feminists, some feminists, use scholarship as a tool?

Yes, they use it for political purposes. At a conference in 1986,
feminist historians adopted a resolution saying that women have an
obligation to see that their scholarship is not used against the interests of women. One of Rosenberg's few supporters at the conference said it's a sad moment in women's history when people can be
accused of being disloyal for telling what they perceive to be the
truth.

With radical feminists, it's not a gentleman's game.

ArLynn Leiber Presser

ArLYNN LEIBER PRESSER is an attorney, novelist and
journalist living in Winnetka, Illinois. At the time of our interview
she was taking a couple of years off from her law practice, which
consisted mainly of divorce, real estate and commercial litigation.
She and her husband have two sons and her husband has joint custody of two children from his previous marriage. ArLynn was born in
1960.

Jack: *When I came across your review of the book* Divorce Reform
at the Crossroads *in the April 1991 American Bar Association Journal, I was heartened by your statement about that book: "While it
proposes to be non-punitive, non-sexist and non-paternalistic, it is precisely punitive and sexist insofar as its focus is on ex-husbands as wrongdoers." Do you think this book is an isolated instance of focusing on
husbands as wrongdoers?*

ArLynn: Absolutely not. Our society has in general looked for
ways to maintain the sexist presumption that divorce occurs when
a male wishes to exit from the relationship for reasons that are
deemed inherently wrong. Legally, we have created no-fault divorce, yet socially we have maintained the presumption of male
fault, especially when we look at treatment of custody and support
issues. I think this is largely because the women's movement is
much more organized and has a much more cohesive ideological
basis than anything going on in the men's movement.

What do you think the ideological basis is?

Largely that our society is a conspiracy of men to maintain power, to maintain material benefit, to maintain prerogative, and that feminism is the way of righting that wrongdoing. That sort of ideological underpinning is seen in a variety of venues, from Naomi Wolf's book about the conspiracy of beauty to how we perceive sex discrimination.

Are male judges, male legislators buying into this male guilt?

They're buying into it, but I don't know that that springs from guilt as much as political reality. With women holding greater than fifty percent of the vote and with women regarded as a feminist voting bloc, I think that male legislators and male judges are very receptive to notions of righting the sexist wrong. It's political unreality in some ways, because when the National Organization for Women or some other like-minded group approaches the legislator or judge, they are claiming to represent a large number of women, when in fact there are groups that counterbalance the feminist group that appear to have larger numbers of members and a greater receptivity within the community at large.

What kind of groups do you mean?

The first group that comes to mind is Concerned Women for America. When NOW speaks, we largely think it is speaking for all women, and we don't tend to think that when CWA raises its voice.

:   Memberships claimed by two women's groups that often take
:   opposing positions: National Organization for Women: 250,000
:   (1991); Concerned Women for America: 600,000 (1992).
:
:
:   USA Today
:   February 4, 1992

Do you think that CWA is any more interested in taking a balanced approach to divorce?

I think that Concerned Women for America has a different idea of divorce from the National Organization for Women, but I don't know that it's based on an idea of gender reconciliation so much as an idea of wanting to maintain family structure for the purposes of child rearing. I think their focus very much is on child issues, education, pornography, abortion, that kind of thing.

If a woman in CWA were in a marriage that she found unhappy and divorce were to result, do you think she would be any less interested in being nonpunitive and nonsexist and nonblaming of men?

I think as a theoretical thing, yes. In the heat of battle, probably no.

> Mrs. Quayle is speaking to the [CWA convention] tonight, and when it was announced that award winners would get to have their pictures taken with her, a great "ooh" sounded in the ballroom. The "essential nature of women," as Quayle put it [during her speech at the 1992 Republican convention], "is to nurture. . . ."
> "I had a very independent life before I got married," said [a CWA member]. "I was an actress, and did public relations for the ski industry in Aspen, and worked at a radio station. But now I stay home and I couldn't be happier."
>
> Megan Rosenfeld
> *Washington Post*
> September 26, 1992

My belief is that both feminist women's groups and conservative women's groups share the idea of women as more virtuous, especially more important in the lives of children.

That is an interesting point and it's probably true.

You mentioned the idea of a male exit from marriage. That conjures the notion of the man running off with his secretary to lead a carefree life while driving a convertible. In those instances where it isn't the man who wants to leave, where it's the man who wants to stay in the marriage, how does standard American ideology work to explain how that's the man's fault, too?

Then we have to run to step B, which is "Well, he must have been doing something in order to make her want to leave." I think we do maintain an extraordinary presumption that if there is violence within a marriage it is male violence directed at females. If there is infidelity within the marriage, it is largely males being unfaithful to females. If there is a chasm between the husband and wife, it is largely the husband's fault.

How did this presumption of male fault arise, and what maintains it?

In the early part of this century we regarded divorce as the female's fault because divorce was such an outrageous and unusual event, and women were regarded, again, as more virtuous, but more virtuous for staying. Now, we maintain it in large part because of an idea of victimization. Our models for victims are primarily women, and we use the law and social constraints to help victims, but we do not recognize how males can be victimized by women.

What are the stereotypes operating against men in divorce?

The stereotype is that men are not interested and should not be interested in taking care of their children after divorce, and the sole measure of a man's involvement with his children after divorce should be in monetary terms. The divorced father is somebody who sees his kids on weekends and who unreliably and inconsistently proffers checks in the interim. In some ways we have created a self-fulfilling prophecy, because when we cast this man out into the cold we still expect him to maintain a high degree of loyalty by sending the check but not by interfering with any decisions that the ex-wife may make with respect to the children. Even though we have said that divorce is something we can easily allow, we still have to come up with a theoretical explanation of why the man should be required to pay a measure of punitive damages for how he has caused the breakup of a marriage.

Are you suggesting that there is an element of punishment in our national attention to child support?

Absolutely. We have an absolute obsession with it. Men who fail to pay child support are bad, but we have absolutely no interest, no attention, no outcry, absolutely nothing when it comes to dads who are shoved away from the family, dads who may not have an opportunity to see their children for long periods of time, dads whose natural male influence as a father has been undermined by his ex-wife. At least here in Illinois, when a woman goes to court and says, "My ex-husband is however many months behind on child support and I want him to pay," if the father comes in and says, "Fine, there is the money issue but let's also talk about the fact that she will not allow me to see the kids and has not allowed me to see the kids for many months," those two issues cannot be joined in a single lawsuit. Interestingly, in every other area of the law, if you have two people who have a dispute about a contractual interaction, all issues are fair game to be joined in a single lawsuit, but you cannot do that with respect to support versus visitation. This is only a small way men are shoved out of the family when it comes to divorce, but it is a very important and very telling point.

What do you think it tells?

I think it tells us that the father-child relationship is so unimportant that we really don't want to deal with it. It is meaningless. Very irrelevant. Fathers are irrelevant but the monetary support is important. I sometimes think that Dan Quayle may have had a point with respect to Murphy Brown. He was not attacking single women. What he was attacking was the idea of fatherhood being irrelevant. He may not be able to complete a sentence, but I think that is what he meant.

Did you see where he later weaseled down?

> Quayle . . . contends his original remarks were intended as "a wake-up call to the deadbeat dads of America" but were distorted by Hollywood "as criticizing single women and single mothers."
>
> Associated Press
> September 22, 1992

That is an interesting thing in itself, that he feels that the only available target is fathers who are failing to pay child support. I am not in any way suggesting that fathers who fail to pay child support are anything less than bad, but it's an easy target. It is easier than complaining that our culture has become very accepting of the idea that fathers are irrelevant.

Are you aware of the statistics of mothers not paying child support when they are ordered to do so?

No. That is a very arcane subject.

> [F]athers who are owed child support are less likely to receive payments [than mothers who are owed support] with 47% receiving nothing, compared to 27% of custodial mothers receiving nothing."
>
> "CUSTODIAL FATHERS: MYTHS, REALITIES AND CHILD SUPPORT POLICY"
> U.S. Department of Health and Human Services
> 1991

The real question, though, would be to ask how compliant with a court order would women be if that order said, "Custody of the children will go to the father. You may visit from time to time. Yet, you will continue to fulfill the traditional female role by going over to your ex-husband and children's house three times a week and cooking, cleaning and shopping for them. And you must leave before the kids come home and you will see the kids only when the husband says it is okay. You owe it to your children."

There would be absolutely no compliance at all. We have decided that that side of the familial commitment can be ignored. It is not part of the equation anymore. We have become very punitive with respect to divorce, custody and support, and so the only issue is male payment.

Some of the terms used by men for getting married imply that men become beasts of burden. "I am getting hitched."

Right. Ball and chain.

I wonder if this has anything to do with why men are sometimes reluctant to pop the big question.

Sure. I think many men have a very real anxiety about marriage. It's stemming from men's fear that it's going to end in divorce or death and it's not clear which one is worse. Women often say men fear commitment because they are immature, they have been coddled, they have been taken care of for so long, that everything is going so wonderfully for them that there is no reason for them to be mature enough to take on the responsibilities of marriage. My contention, though, is that men are looking over a cliff and they see lots of possible ways they can screw up being married and they don't want to make that plunge.

In seeking redress for antimale biases in divorce, where is the middle ground for men? We don't want to suggest that men should sit and wring their hands and say, "Oh, poor us, we are victims. Somebody fix this problem for us." But on the other hand, we don't want men to continue in typical, macho denial: "I got no problems that I can't handle on my own." Or denial could also cause a guy, upon hearing that his buddy got screwed in divorce, to think, "I didn't know about my buddy, but he must have been doing something terrible. Certainly that could never happen to me!" What do you think would be a more healthy response on the part of men, somewhere between passive denial and passive wallowing in victimhood?

Yes, I don't think I can bear it if another group joins the cacophony of victimhood. I am really unsure about where men can go. Men do not open up to each other to the degree that women open up to other women. It's much easier to get a group of women to come together and find a common ground emotionally and then get them to go out and do something about it. That, I think, would be sort of the starting point, but I don't see that as happening in our country right now.

The current wisdom is that women talk to other women because they are interested in relationships and community, while men are interested in competition and hierarchy. I understand that and I think there is probably some truth to it . . .

I absolutely disagree with that. I think that what happens is that men largely have a degree of confidence about their strength and about their ability to move events. Women largely have only the confidence of their words. Their words are basically their only weapons, so I think that the reason why women are more cohesive in talking about feelings is that those are their strengths, those are their strong points.

Let me suggest the other spin I think we could put on this whole thing. When I was a little boy and I heard that my parents' friends were getting divorced, I had the very clear impression that divorce was always the man's fault. That made me feel bad about men. Only later did I realize that the reason I thought that divorce was always the man's fault was because it was only the women who were talking about it. We could say that women talk, not so much to build community, but—you used the word weapons, I would say tools—to use words as tools to shape public perception of ambiguous events.

Vera said: "Why do you feel you have to turn everything into a story?"

So I told her why:

Because if I tell the story, I control the version.

NORA EPHRON
in *Heartburn*,
her semi-fictional novel of her failed marriage to journalist Carl Bernstein

Men, on the other hand, know that to discuss a personal matter is inevitably going to be self-serving, and I think there is an element of nobility in men that wishes to avoid being self-serving at the expense of another, especially "the mother of my children."

That is very interesting. What strikes me is that when a man does that, if indeed that is what men are doing, his behavior has a very real and valuable function in terms of survival of the species and survival of the community as a whole. The problem is how you get from that point to pushing men toward either political or social solutions for their issues.

Tell me what you see as being the survival function here.

I don't think that marriage developed as a male plot to get women to run the microwave. I think that marriage developed because there is a need to protect women from public conflict, to keep women protected so that they can concentrate their energy on educating the young, feeding the young, pushing the young toward adulthood. Humans have an enormously long period of helpless childhood. To have a sort of primal male feeling of always owing allegiance to "the mother of my children" is something without which we really couldn't have gotten society rolling. When women go to the mat on divorce and when they use their children against their husbands, they do themselves a disservice, because they don't key into the very natural loyalty that he may feel. It could benefit children by having their father working in cooperation with the ex-wife. Instead of calling his ex-wife "the witch," he might be calling her "the mother of my children," which has a much better ring to it. I think it would benefit the husband himself, the ex-husband, in that he can have a relationship with his children that is not tinged with guilt and anxiety.

The image you painted of the man wanting to protect the mother of his children is very powerful. It's often alleged that men want relationships with their children after divorce only as a bargaining chip so that they can lower their child support payments. I am sure there is some truth to that. What do you think of the possibility that sometimes women want custody of their kids after divorce only because they know that having custody of the kids after divorce is their reason to be protected and supported?

Absolutely. I also think society regards ex-wives who do not have custody of their children as being somehow horrible. "My God, what did she do to lose custody of her kids?"

In some ways then, women who really don't want custody of their kids . . .

Or who want to share custody . . .

. . . or who think the husband could be better for the kid right now, are forced into taking custody?

Yes. I think we need to set up more social support and legal support for parents who want to be more creative with custody solutions.

It's certainly a good idea for men to recognize and respect the importance of the mother of their children. What about men demanding that women recognize and respect the importance of the father of their children?

At the request of my husband, Carl Bernstein ("Carl"), I hereby agree . . . that I will do everything within my power to see that no harm is caused to our children as the result of the publication of the Book [*Heartburn*] or a movie based upon the Book. This is especially true in terms of possible harm that might be caused the children through . . . misinformation about . . . their parents' marriage, separation, divorce, and roles as parents. . . . [Some of the events described in the Book] are totally of my own invention and have no basis in fact. These include any and all scenes in the Book from which any inference might be drawn that Carl has ever been less than a caring, loving and conscientious father. . . . This is especially the case in regard to a scene in the Book in which the father . . . demonstrates an attitude of inattention and disconcern toward his son during an illness. . . . I will exercise my best efforts to prevent any such scene from appearing in a movie.

from Attachment A to the Marital Separation Agreement between Nora Ephron and Carl Bernstein as published in *Harper's Magazine* September 1985

Again, I think there are some natural barriers to men communicating with each other and communicating with women about their needs, either legal, political, social or emotional. There is also the question of how do men manage to do this without being accused of being horrors, conservatives or reactionary.

Any thoughts on that?

I see this as an intractable problem, sort of unsolvable, sort of like Rubik's Cube, just not something that is solvable.

Does it look like there is no hope?

Not that there is no hope, but there will have to be some incredible social shifts in order for it to occur.

The great social shift that I think is the only hope is that women need to say to men—because men are not going to say it to themselves—"Hey, guys, we recognize we need you. We recognize your value. We recognize your importance. We want to make amends for some of the attitudes that we have had—and that we have helped you to inculcate—about your importance in this society beyond the merely economic." That's the hope of this book. What do you think?

I think the book can be a good launching point, but I think it is not going to bring us all the way home. Books have sort of a half-life in people's imagination. You are swimming against the tide. The popular culture has it that men are jerks, women are virtuous.

That's it. We just need an awareness, it just has to become the cool thing to stop beating up on men. It has to become the cool thing for men to stand up and claim some dignity. And it has to be a cool thing for women to want that kind of man.

Maybe what you need is a shift to it being cool to recognize male needs. I don't know that that is a big trend right now.

Right. And when it comes to gender stylishness, the arbiters are clearly women. Women could say, "Hey, from now on the fashion is going to be that the men who take this nonsense lying down will be vilified as wimps." Then I think men would say, "I certainly don't want women to think I'm a wimp. I'd better wake up!"
I am optimistic, aren't I?

Very.

Ellen Dublin Levy

ELLEN DUBLIN LEVY is the secretary of the Children's Rights Council, a national organization founded by Ellen's husband David. CRC works for family formation and family preservation, and if parents divorce, to ensure that children have the opportunity to maintain relationships with both parents. David has a sixteen-year-old son, Justin, from his first marriage. Ellen and David have a seven-year-old daughter Diana. Ellen has worked extensively in day care as a teacher and director, and now works for a Prince George's County (Maryland) agency that provides referrals for parents seeking child care and training for providers and parents.

Jack: *What is the main change you would advocate in women's ideas, their ideas of men, and their ideas about relationships between women and men?*

Ellen: The main change is that we need to compromise. We need to trust each other more, because right now we really are men versus women, women versus men. We do think that way. Women do and men do. If we can find a little more middle ground, we can probably continue to get along in the ways we're getting along well—which are many—but we may also find ways to get beyond men versus women.

What are the ways in which we're not getting along well.

We don't trust each other's judgment.

On any particular issue?

On almost anything. Women think they know how to take care of babies better. Men think they can drive a car better. On almost anything you mention, you could say, "That's men's territory" or "That's women's territory."

We know that keeping women out of men's territory is wrong because it's unfair to women. I wonder if you could talk about some unfairnesses toward men, about men's desire to enter women's territory.

It is fraught with difficulty. Men are talking about taking care of children, staying home, not being committed to being the sole breadwinner. But it's still difficult for a man.

Do women enjoy their primacy in the lives of children, generally speaking?

Yes.

What kind of enjoyment do they get out of it? What do women get out of primacy in the lives of children?

For many women it is the justification of their existence. *Fulfilled* is a word you would often hear.

Thirty years ago a male bricklayer would have said, "My craft is my fulfillment, this is my existence, this is my life, this is what makes me a man." And he might have resisted a woman wanting to do the same job. I'm wondering if many women have invested their idea of womanhood, their idea of being feminine and female, in raising their kids. Is there any level on which women wish to avoid what the bricklayer wished to avoid, seeing a person of another gender doing what he thought only a person of his gender could do?

I'm sure that's very much at the heart of the problem men face.

It was a mistake for the women's movement to say that the bricklayer was a chauvinist pig, to berate him and ridicule him and to be generally mean to him, rather than to say, "I understand where the guy's coming from." How could we in a nice way say to women, "We understand where you're coming from, but you've got to open up the trade union here"?

I think the trade union is opening up. We do see fathers taking care of their children, we do see women bricklayers, and we do see both parents as caring, affectionate, nurturing people in their children's lives, much more now than we ever did before. I think that people see Bill and Hillary Clinton as caring parents. He seems like he really is an involved father.

Is that threatening to women in the way that seeing women making it in a man's domain was threatening to men?

I think it is even more threatening in one's own home where it really does threaten the balance of power. One of the things that is involved here is power. I see and hear and feel a lot of resentment toward fathers after divorce. A lot of the men David knows and hears from didn't initiate their divorces. However, there's a lot of feeling that once there is a divorce, the father was the one who didn't care about the family, that if he shows interest he has an ulterior motive; and no matter how clearly he states his feelings—"I miss my children, I want to be with them, I want to be a part of their growing up"—they're often attacked, or misinterpreted, or not heard.

Are they not heard despite an earnest attempt and a desire on the part of society to hear them, or are they not heard because who cares, to hell with the father?

It's as though they were the father but they are not the father anymore. I really think that we understand deep in our heart and deep in our spirit the importance of fathers and what a father means to a child, but those of us who become mothers often find it hard to acknowledge what we knew as daughters. And so we've separated out a class of fathers.

What class of fathers have we separated out?

The ones who have left the home.

So we feel justified in saying, "Because he left, we know he doesn't care."

Yes.

Do you understand the fallacy of that assumption?

Yes. He would be not very well accepted if he said, "This is the house that I built and now that my wife and I are separating, I'm staying here with the children and she's going."

And so is it a lack of caring that causes him to uproot himself? Or can it sometimes be a manifestation of caring?

It can be a manifestation of caring and a manifestation of doing what is socially acceptable. But once you do it, you are practically relinquishing your parental rights.

I once saw a cartoon of a man running out of his house with his clothes on fire. The mother was standing in the doorway with the kid in her arms saying "See? That proves he doesn't care about you." Why do you think we're so ready to assume that if he leaves it's an indication of something bad about the father?

Probably because his generation started out as the head of that household. We may function like a matriarchal society in many ways, mostly having to do with family life and child-related matters, but we think we are a patriarchal society.

Which is more influential, the reality or the figment of our imaginations?

It depends. It depends what gets reinforced. Probably the reality of everyday life. But it also depends what other people say and think.

If a woman were to run out of an office building unhappy after having been fired, would our automatic assumption be that she didn't care about her job?

Not necessarily.

Then why are we so ready to assume the man didn't care about his family?

I wish I knew.

One of the points you started with is the idea of trust. What is it that we do not trust men to be and to do?

"We" being we women?

We women, we as a society.

I'll start with we women. In a relationship, we don't trust men to be loyal, faithful, interested.

Could we call this suspicion, this lack of trust, could we call this any kind of prejudice, or bias, or even bigotry?

I suppose that we grow up with a feeling bordering on contempt of men, of boys will be boys. A good man is hard to find. It's a judgmental way of thinking that we learn from the time we're little girls—to be careful.

> What bothers me most, however, is the visible, although often unspoken, thread of contempt that runs through women's conversations about men. The assumption very often is that men are boys who must be outfoxed, manipulated or dealt with in a calculated manner that women rarely use among themselves.
>
> PHYLLIS THEROUX
> GQ
> February 1986

If a little boy were told to be careful of little girls, that would smack of a whole different motivation toward girls than telling girls to be careful of boys. Telling a girl to be careful of a boy seems to be prudent. Telling boys to be careful of girls seems to be something else.

Yes.

What does it seem to be?

Unnecessary (*laughter*).

What would you think of a father who said to his sons, "Be careful of girls. You can not trust them." What would we think about a guy like that?

That he had a very serious problem, that he hated women. He had a problem.

Why is it that the woman who tells the daughter to be careful of boys isn't seen as having a problem? Is it because boys do bad things and girls don't do bad things?

No.

What is it then? We want men to express themselves, but if a man dares to express any distrust of women, any bad experience with women, we smack him back down by calling him a woman-hater. Are women less willing to acknowledge their faults and foibles than men are?

> **misogyny** (fear, hatred or distrust of women):
> "a widely accepted social attitude in a sexist world."
> includes beliefs that "demean [women's] bodies . . . abilities . . . characters and . . . efforts."
> **misandry** (fear, hatred or distrust of men):
> "1) a refusal to suppress the evidence of one's experience with men; 2) a woman's defense against fear and pain; 3) an affirmation of the cathartic effects of justifiable anger."
>
> from *A Feminist Dictionary*
> compiled by Cheris Kramarae and Paula Treichler

Women are very willing to acknowledge their faults and foibles to women friends and gay men friends.

Whether it's so or not, most women feel that men have the upper hand. Now you may think, "Well you're just saying that, Ellen, but inwardly you know that you have a lot of control, that you have a lot of influence in how you conduct your family life." And inwardly I may know that and I may even discuss it openly with friends, but I don't think that many woman are really convinced that they have the upper hand.

Fair enough. Would it come as any great surprise to you that I don't know many men who think, especially in their dealings with women, that they have the upper hand?

No. I guess not.

Would you quarrel with my thought that it is much easier for women to express their feelings of powerlessness vis-à-vis men that it is for men to express their feelings of powerlessness vis-à-vis women?

No, I think that's a very good point. I can understand that.

You mentioned that with your friends you might talk openly about the ways in which women have power and the ways in which women have the upper hand. But that was only with your friends. In this book let's say we're all among friends. Can you talk openly here about the kinds of power women have?

I could. But because I've probably never done it, I don't know where to begin.

Okay, so have you never done this with your women friends, never talked about the kinds of power and influence and control that women have?

I think that when we do it, the way that we would do it would be to say how successfully we may have deceived—or think that we have deceived—our husband or our mate.

Is that a main element of women's control and power?

The power to deceive men is the first thing that comes to my mind. I think women have that power, or at least are taught to act as if we do. And men seem to go along with the act.

How do women justify deceiving men?

Part of it is that women know what they want, or think they know what they want, but they're not sure they would get it by being direct. I can think of a wonderful example in my own life because it's so recent. I had to make a decision and I didn't think David was going to have any input, but he did and his input resulted in a much better outcome. Diana was going to start music lessons and I had decided that the best thing to do was just to get an electronic keyboard rather than repair our old piano. I knew that David would prefer a piano, but I didn't think that he would object. But he did object. He started asking people how they felt about pianos and keyboards, and he concluded that he did not want Diana to start out on a keyboard. But piano lessons were starting in four days. I felt like I wanted to be in charge of this. I had found the piano teacher and I almost wanted to insist. If he hadn't said anything or if I could have gotten away with it, I would have just gone out and gotten a keyboard and then worked toward getting a piano. By now Diana had taken sides with me that she wanted a keyboard, because that's what she's seen. After her first lesson on a piano, she said "Okay. Piano." And by now I was able to say to David, "You're right, honey." It's not easy for me to say that when it has to do with our daughter.

If he had not injected himself, if he had not crashed through that barrier, is it possible that the decision could have been made and you could have thought he didn't care?

Sure.

Was the fact that this decision involved Diana at all connected with the fact that you wanted this to be your decision?

Yes.

Do you in your heart of hearts have any thought that when it comes to Diana you are more important than David is?

Oh, sure. And yet I know that might not be so for Diana. I also know that I see myself undermining her relationship with her father, interfering with it, doing everything that women who undermine father-child relationships after a divorce are guilty of doing. I see myself doing it in a family that I cherish. I am devoted to David and I really do appreciate the kind of father he is to Justin and Diana in many ways that are so clear to me. And I don't know anything more beautiful really than the relationship David has with Justin.

How does it compare in beauty to the relationship David has with Diana?

That's very interesting. It's equally beautiful in a different way. But he has much more of a barrier, ironically. Honestly he has much more of a barrier in his relationship to Diana than he does in his relationship to Justin. I don't think it's because Justin is a boy and Diana is a girl. I think it's because he has worked things through with Justin's mother through sheer agonizing, gut-wrenching trial and error, and time. They have worked so hard at it that he has a more equal partnership with Justin's mother in the raising of Justin than he has with me in the raising of Diana. And that's something I really need to work on because . . . it's true.

Why do you undermine David's relationship with Diana?

I certainly don't do it on purpose. I do it because I'm so attached to her. I feel very fortunate to have married David, to have Justin and Diana. I don't let him have enough of her. That's the main thing. I keep her much too much to me. I had Diana when I was almost forty. A few minutes after Diana was born I felt as if I had always known her. I continue to feel that way.

Do you have any idea how that compares with feelings that David might have about her? Does David perhaps feel that he has known Diana forever?

I don't know. I never thought of asking him. I think that he sees his children, however much they remind me and others of him, as separate entities.

[Bill Clinton] is a wonderful father. He's always been very sensitive to Chelsea and her needs and very aware of what she was going through. But I don't think that most men—even the ones whom I admire as fathers, like my husband—have their children's needs in mind all the time. I think that they're able to compartmentalize their lives more than women are able to. I really do think it's something that is part of our makeup. I don't know whether it's biological or social.

In my own experience, I've worked with many, many men in many different settings, and nearly every one I ever worked with was, I thought, a devoted and caring and committed father, but it wasn't something that they carried with them full-time. It wasn't something that was always on their minds.

HILLARY RODHAM CLINTON
quoted by Roxanne Roberts
Redbook
March 1993

Let's assume that you're right, that David sees them as separate entities and that you see them as an extension of yourself in some way, as circles inside of your circle perhaps.

Yes.

Do you see your concept of parenthood being in any way better than David's concept of parenthood?

I see it as safer.

Do you see safer as better? Do you see safer as always better?

I always see safer as better when it comes to taking care of children.

I'm wondering whether you assume that your style of being a parent is the style that Diana most needs and therefore justifies your making it primary and screening out David's to some extent.

Are you asking do I honestly think that Diana needs my style of parenting? Oh, no, I don't honestly think that. I think that *I* need it.

And so your undermining David is more for you than for Diana?

Yes.

Do you see the possibility that there might be many women who are not quite as aware or as open or as honest as you are and who would insist, "Oh no no no, I undermine the father's relationship with the kids not for myself but for the children."

- Only about one mother in four thought that fathers should play a fifty-fifty role in raising the children.
- Mothers want fathers to help more with the children, but not to overshadow their role as primary parent.
- Two out of three mothers seemed threatened by the idea of a father's equal participation in child rearing.
- Mothers themselves may be subtly putting a damper on men's involvement with their children because they are so possessive of their role as primary nurturer.

> *The Motherhood Report*
> Louis Genevie, Ph.D., and Eva Margolies
> 1987

For that matter—and I'm not talking about instances where children have to be protected from one or the other parent—I would say that many people wouldn't consider it undermining.

Might they consider it simply something that should happen in the natural order of things? "I'm the mother. I am the mother."

Oh sure. I feel that way, and my husband is the head of a national organization on shared parenting. It's confusing. I should step back and give David and Diana the chance to be father and daughter, separate from me. But David has told me very, very often that he's happy and grateful that I'm so very concerned about Justin and interested in him, and I think it's very reassuring for David.

Let me take us back to the piano decision and the barrier David had to get over to get into that decision. What would have happened if David didn't have the courage, power, strength and the conviction to get over the barrier?

He would have felt left out. He wouldn't have shared as much in the joy and pride of Diana's first recital—when we get there.

Sandra Rippey

SANDRA RIPPEY holds the rank of commander after eighteen years in the U.S. Naval Reserve. As a reservist, she serves two weeks of active duty with the Navy each year. She is married to an active-duty Navy senior chief petty officer and was previously married to a Marine Corps aviator. Her father was a career Army officer. She was born in 1947, and lives in Canaan, New Hampshire. The views she expresses here are hers, not the Navy's. In making these statements, Commander Rippey does not represent the Navy or anyone in the Navy other than herself.

Jack: *For those of us who might not know the significance of "commander," could you run through the Navy's order of promotions?*

Sandra: In the Navy, an officer starts out as an ensign, then lieutenant junior grade, lieutenant, lieutenant commander, commander, captain, then admiral.

So in two years you'll have a shot at captain, and then, possibly, admiral?

That's right.

I first found you through a letter you wrote to the editor of the Valley News *of Lebanon, New Hampshire, not too far from your home. What motivated your letter?*

As you know, there was a convention of naval aviators who are members of what's called the Tailhook Association. It is—or was—an annual event that takes place in Las Vegas. Apparently, there was some abuse of some of the women. The editorial in the *Valley News*, however, was written by some civilians looking at that incident, about which they knew nothing. They referred to the demeaning and demanding things that women in the military must endure—aside from basic training—and how terribly they're treated. I simply felt compelled to state the facts.

> The 1991 Tailhook Convention is a small event on the grand scale of sexual discrimination and mistreatment of women in the military. . . . It's a given that women trying to build careers in the military face fears and obstacles much greater than basic training.
>
> "The Tailhook Mess"
> an editorial in the *Valley News*
> Lebanon, New Hampshire
> September 26, 1992

I simply wanted to address the issue and state that this is not really the case. I'm living proof that one can succeed simply by doing a good job. I've been tested to the limits of my professional ability. Early on in my career there was some good-natured ribbing. But once you do a job, all of that goes away.

My women contemporaries and I are doing fine, for the most part. We've been through it. Over the years we've been assimilated into the community. But as I stated in my article, one of the more insidious things that's happening is that women officers junior to me will address the issue of sexual harassment as the first thing they want to talk about—how terrible the men are, how badly they've been treated, how they didn't get promoted, their assignments are no good. That's how they open up conversations with me, simply because of my gender. The worst thing about it is that they will not consider evidence to the contrary. I cannot talk to these women and tell them, "You're wrong. Give the guys a chance. Work with them. Do your job. Just maintain." Their zeal is almost religious. I see it among enlisted women as well as female officers, but mostly I see it among the officers. Now, I want to make clear that not all the young women are like this, but still the problem is significant and pervasive.

What does this zeal do for them? Why do they cling to it?

It's a bizarre phenomenon that I watch, basically, as an outsider. These women all share a loathing. There's no place in it for me, but they seem to almost feed on it. The men, for their part, see this gaggle of individuals who are sharply separated from them by these feelings. It's a coming-apart of a community, the officer community. I'm not pleased with it at all.

> Male aviators told [a Congressional hearing] that letting women fly in combat squadrons would be disruptive. Lt. John Claget, an F/A-18 fighter pilot who flew during the Persian Gulf war, said he didn't doubt there are women who can fly fighter jets in combat. But, he said, "When a guy's made an obvious mistake, he will get a finger in the chest. It's very personal. . . . I am not able to give that direct feedback to a woman."
>
> NAVY TIMES
> August 24, 1992

Does it seem that perhaps the women who are operating this way are looking for a weapon to beat their way to the top?

I think what they're looking for is a vehicle. I hate to say this, but these women are looking for a vehicle to skip the steps. In other words, the men have to go through certain gradations to their Surface Warfare pin, or their Submarine pin, or their Aviator wings. The women are looking for and being granted shortcuts only because they're women. This is wrong. There is resentment in the male community because of this. The resentment is not unwarranted.

How do you know the men are resentful?

Because I talk to them.

What do they say?

They say that because of the way these steps are "dumbed down" for the women, it degrades and makes less valuable the increased time that the men have to put in to acquire the same qualifications or promotions. And they do resent it. I live with them and talk with them and interact with them freely, and they know that they are free to speak with me at all times. I hear it all, which makes me a kind of unique conduit in understanding what's rumbling on the male side and what's rumbling on the female side.

In your letter to the editor you described a sexual harassment training . . .

That was required Navy-wide. It was a one day stand-down for all hands.

Can you describe what happened during that day?

We were shown a series of three videotapes that had been produced by the Navy to illustrate what they meant by sexual harassment. And then there was a facilitator who had been trained to give the harassment training. The videotapes cast the typical male service member as basically this brutish predator who at all times would stare at, look at, suggest sex to any female in his vicinity. The man looked like a prowling tomcat, which I didn't appreciate. The videos didn't apply to any situations that I've ever seen. And I thought that the level of sensitivity among the women was already so high that they were walking around like raw wounds waiting to be stuck.

Did any of the videos ever show any objectionable behavior on the part of the women?

No.

The women were never portrayed as doing anything wrong?

Never. After the videos, we had a little discussion group. That was fine until one young woman in the back of the room, I think she was a junior officer, raised her hand and she said, "You know what training we really need? Women in the Navy need to be trained to be more sensitive to sexual harassment." As if you don't know when you're harassed!

What was the response to that suggestion?

A sort of mushy, noncommittal response from the facilitator. Most everyone else in the room rolled their eyes.

As if to say, "The last thing we need is more sensitivity, hypersensitivity"?

That's right. I think the final issue that caused me just to shut down and say, "Okay, that's it!" was when they were talking about feminist legal theorists and one of the women raised her hand to say, "All sex is rape, even sex in marriage."

When she said all sex is rape, what she was saying is that whenever there is sex, a man is raping a woman.

That's right.

Is it even conceivable that a man could stand up and say, "Excuse me, but when you say such things, you are sexually harassing me."

I wish someone would have. I wish one of the guys would have stood up.

What did these guys do?

They just went blank. There's no avenue for the men to be able to counter this. That's why I'm not sitting still any longer. That's why I'll address every one of these issues, because no one can claim that I have an agenda because of my gender. If a man said the same things that I am saying, there would be an outcry.

Let's imagine that the sociopolitical climate in the Navy were much healthier than it is. What would the men say if they felt free to speak?

Equal pay for equal work, period! We're all treated the same. No exceptions. None. And I fully agree with that.

What would they say about sexual harassment? What would they say about the videos they were required to watch? What would they say about the attitudes of the women you described earlier?

They would be offended by the videos, that we wrongly portray the typical Navy man as a marauding tomcat ready to pounce on any convenient female target. Men aren't like that. They would be offended. They should be able to say that they were offended.

And if a guy were to stand up and say, "I'm offended by the imbalance of all this," what would happen to him in today's climate?

He'd be hooted down. He be hooted down by the female population in the room.

Is it likely that the female population might make sure that his horrible behavior would be noted on his fitness report?

Good question. I don't know that that would be the case for a few more years, but indeed that could happen. I see it coming.

What would happen in a few more years to make this possible?

When these junior females come into positions of leadership, I can see where they will demand conformity, and any exceptions whatsoever will be noted somewhere in their fitness reports.

I understand that part of an officer's evaluation is how well he or she embraces Navy policy on these issues.

Yes, that's right.

Now if a male officer says, "I'm sorry, but I disagree with our approach to sexual harassment here," would that be officially marked on his report as a negative rating?

Yes. That's why they don't say it. It would be shown in the marks on the front, or somewhere in the narrative on the back.

Now this would be his superior, commanding officer grading him on these things?

Yes.

Is there assurance for the men that if they speak on these issues they will be treated fairly?

No. None.

What are they apprehensive about?

As soon as they address an issue, like women on ships, women in submarines, as soon as they address the issue, practically speaking, the hue and cry of sexism rears its ugly head and shuts them up.

Is this purely on a peer level, on a social level rather than an official chain of command?

On both levels. That's what's so disheartening.

Is it possible that some women in the military might come in with unhealthy, limiting, narrow, destructive and sexist ideas about men?

Sure.

Is anybody addressing that?

No.

Is there any effort at all to ask women to examine their behavior or their attitudes about the opposite sex?

Except for the forum of this sexual harassment lecture, no.

And the forum of the sexual harassment lecture, is that manifestly a balanced presentation?

In my opinion, no. I think that one of the videos ought to have shown a female lieutenant and a chief, for example, with her giving him a problem. There was no such balance.

The chief is below her in the chain of command?

That's right.

Does it ever happen that way?

Absolutely. There was a female lieutenant commander fired at the Pentagon for doing exactly that.

But they couldn't talk about that in the videos.

No.

Let me try to figure out why somebody wants this to be happening. Here's my theory. You've got a group that feels itself in competition with another group, and rather than working hard to be as good as the other group, they decide to chop this other group down, to demoralize it, to shame it, to cripple it.

That's entirely possible, yes. I see it happening.

Do you see the group of men in this example being actually affected by this campaign?

To the extent that they cannot be honest with their counterparts, to the extent that they can not fraternize with their own peers, men are shell-shocked in the military. They're spending so much time running and ducking for cover and looking over their shoulders waiting for the next incoming round that yes, it is demoralizing for them.

So somebody wants them to be on the defensive?

Well, they are. The campaign is working.

Do you think that maybe Tailhook wasn't what we've been told it was? Do you think maybe the media are caught up in the emotion of it all? That's happened before, you know. Remember the way the media handled the hazing of that female midshipman at the Naval Academy? It started out balanced and reasonable, but now it's another Navy horror story.

In interviews, several midshipmen said that although what happened to [Naval Academy student Gwen] Dreyer was unusual because the men who handcuffed her were of a higher rank, it was not extremely different from common occurrences. For example, they said that upperclassmen are often tied to chairs and put outside or have their heads put in toilets as retaliation by plebes they command. They also doubt Dreyer was targeted because she is a woman, but instead think the episode, while wrong, grew out of Dreyer's involvement in a spirited snowball fight.

LISA LEFF
Washington Post
May 30, 1990

Dreyer was chained to a urinal in a men's room before a jeering crowd of her male classmates.

MOLLY MOORE
Washington Post
July 19, 1990

I think that's entirely possible. I know what Tailhook is. I was married to a Tailhooker. I have a friend who was at Tailhook. I know what happens there. But let me also say that there are women in California, Nevada, Arizona, New Mexico who save all year long to go to Tailhook, to party with the aviators. That's their whole mission in life. And they love it. They have a blast. I don't know what happened. They are still allegations at this point.

> Four California women who visited Tailhook Association conventions in 1990 and '91 have sued the association and the Las Vegas Hilton, saying they were sexually accosted by Navy aviators attending the events. . . .
>
> Federal tort claims filed with the Navy last week seek in excess of $2.5 million on behalf of each woman. . . .
>
> [One California woman] alleges in her lawsuit that she was "sexually accosted and molested" on Sept. 8, 1990, by "numerous Naval personnel." . . .
>
> [Her] lawsuit said she returned to the convention in 1991, believing the incidents of 1990 wouldn't be repeated.
>
> ROBERT MACY
> Associated Press
> September 9, 1992

There seems to be an attempt to shame the entire Tailhook Association. Actually, it seems like an attempt to shame the entire Navy or even to shame all men.

Yes, that had occurred to me.

Do you think the American people need to be careful that we don't have a witch hunt going on here?

We have had one already. There have been admirals' heads rolling. The Navy has gotten absolutely torched by this.

Tell me how the Navy "dumbs down" its requirements for women.

Surface Warfare qualification is a very good example. It takes the men probably a solid three or four months at sea with one liberty break, busting their butts with the books, taking their "qual" cards, going through all these different board levels up to their commanding officer to get their SWO—Surface Warfare Officer—pin. Women, on the other hand, have been known to be awarded the SWO pin in their spare time. There was a gal out in San Diego who was going to law school, drilling aboard a ship in the evenings, in port, in the harbor, and she got her qualification in about six weeks. It's not right. A full-court press has been put on to equalize men and women. It's basically a quota thing. You've got to crank out so many woman. And they're doing it in the most expeditious manner that they can find. If we're striving for equal pay for equal work, this is not it. And as a female, I don't want that. Make me do what they do. There should be no difference in the requirements. If you can't meet them, you're out. But I'm a lone voice crying in the wilderness here.

> [Barbara Spyridon] Pope was chairwoman of an ad hoc committee on Navy women in the wake of the scandal over the 1991 Tailhook Convention. . . . Ms. Pope's committee recommended in early January [1993] . . . that all naval combat jobs be opened to women except for those likely to involve "hand-to-hand combat." . . . "All of this grew out of Tailhook," Ms. Pope said. "As we looked at assimilation and integration of women, combat exclusions and how we do business, it was clear women had been made to feel like second-class citizens."
>
> RICHARD H. P. SIA
> *Baltimore Sun*
> April 2, 1993

Now if men are pulling away from women, are women also perhaps being harmed by not having the men available to coach them, teach them, show them?

Absolutely, they're being deprived. They're being deprived of a number of things. You can only get technical skills by osmosis, from being around and doing it. They're also missing social skills, the way you interact with your counterparts. They're being deprived of seeing good leadership. If you're going to be a good leader, you've got to see it happening and incorporate that. Absolutely. They're missing it.

Tell me about the reaction you received from your letter to the editor.

I'm well-known enough around the upper valley in New Hampshire, at the post office, the bank, the local store, the bowling alley, multiples of people, I'd say a dozen and a half or so came up to me and said, "Right on! It's about time somebody said that!"

Men and women?

Men and women! Nothing negative. I didn't get a single negative response.

Now this is in New Hampshire. Skeptics might say, "Well, New Hampshire is very conservative and they're out of touch."

I also sent photocopies to a number of people from around the country and I got the same reaction. Men and women.

Why do we get the impression from the general media, from reading news stories and magazine articles, that women are all contrary to the point of view you represent?

Beats me. There's a hidden agenda there that I haven't actually been able to put square corners on yet.

What do you like about men?

I think men generally are very warm and caring individuals. What I have found, of late, particularly, is that when they find a woman like myself to whom they can address these issues and other personal issues, they're astonished.

Does it seem then that one of the reasons guys don't talk with women is not just that men have trouble talking, but that sometimes women have trouble listening?

Yes, absolutely. Because a woman hears from a man what she allows him to say. In other words, by her body language, by what she puts out, she's only going to hear what he reads and he sends back on the same frequency. If you're more open, and more accepting, and nonjudgmental, you'll hear the whole range of what this guy has to say. And it's quite diverse.

So you're talking about the ability of women to fairly thoroughly control what a guy will say.

Basically they do. Yes.

So where does this idea come from that women have no power?

Oh, that's the oldest, stupidest idea that's ever been conveyed. Women control what men say. Women control sex. Women control procreation. The whole idea is bogus.

It makes sense that women aren't going to stand up and say, "Hey, this idea that's been benefiting us is bogus."

That's right.

Why aren't men standing up and saying, "Hey, this idea that's hurting us is bogus!"?

Sexist!

If a guy were to say that, he would be accused of being a sexist?

Absolutely.

Does it disappoint you that men are taking this stuff?

Yeah. A little bit. But they've been so battered for the last ten years. I don't see that they have a choice at this point. Every time somebody does stand up, they get knocked down like a bowling pin. And there's just so much of that you can take. And I can see that there's a certain tired acquiescence on the part of men.

Not exactly an emotion we should want in our military, is it?

Tired acquiescence? Not if we ever want to win a war.

Elizabeth Herron

ELIZABETH HERRON is an educator and consultant in women's empowerment and gender reconciliation. She has led numerous women's groups and taught university courses on gender issues. She is the mother of two daughters, has been divorced, and is now in a committed relationship with Aaron Kipnis, Ph.D., with whom she is authoring *Gender War, Gender Peace* (Morrow, February 1994). She is codirector of the Santa Barbara Institute for Gender Studies, conducting gender reconciliation trainings nationwide. Liz was born in 1952.

Jack: *You've said that, contrary to popular belief, women are powerful. The popular belief, then, is that women are not powerful?*

Elizabeth: I think the popular paradigm right now is that women have been denied access to power. It's been a developmental stage for women as a collective to recognize that we've lost something and that we need to find it. We've assumed in that equation that because we've lost it, men have it. But men are starting to speak up now—Aaron does it in his book *Knights Without Armor*—about the ways they don't feel powerful, either.

What would some of those ways be?

I'll just mention a few. Men experience that they are not treated fairly around the issues of child custody. There's a lot of pain in that. A big issue for men is the current scapegoating of men and masculinity. The lack of available social services for men—most of the homeless people on the streets are men, many of them are Vietnam veterans. If a woman begins to fall through the cracks, she has more access to social services than a man does. Men are dying on the job twenty to one over women. Men are also asking for their culture—not just corporate, economic culture—to be studied in the same way that female culture has been studied recently through women's studies programs in universities.

You and Aaron work on creating partnership between men and women. How can we be partners in a patriarchy?

I take issue with the whole notion of describing our social system as a patriarchy. We see the damage that's been done by our dominant cultural system, but calling it a patriarchy connects it solely with masculinity and men. I don't believe that's really an adequate description of what we have. Our culture has more to do with a class system in which both men and women have participated. This dominant culture does not represent masculine culture any more than it represents feminine culture.

Many feminists will insist that only men benefit from what they—the more polarized feminists—will insist on calling patriarchy. To help balance the picture, could we talk about ways in which women benefit from the dominant culture?

Technology has created problems, but it has benefited us all. We all like our modern conveniences. We are not real fond of taking our clothes to the nearest stream and pounding them on rocks. And by working in the outside world, men have given women the opportunity to stay home with children. Now, you could say that women have been imprisoned by that. But you could also say that women have the freedom to have deep intimacy with children, which is something that men feel is denied to them by virtue of their provider role.

Is society matriarchal in any important ways?

Yes. Women are still the primary parents of children. You know that saying, The hand that rocks the cradle rules the world. In most relationships that I see between men and women, women are in charge of the emotional dynamics of the relationship. In the whole arena of relationships, women dominate. We're painting with a broad brush here, we're making generalizations, but I think that, to a large degree, it's true. We often find that it's the woman who organizes the social life of the family or of the relationship. It's women who are keeping little bonds going all over the place—in the PTA, clubs, churches and other kinds of social activities.

What if I were to say "Oh, that's not important stuff!"?

I would disagree with you. I couldn't prove it to you scientifically, but if we look at who runs families, who runs the emotional life of families, who has the power when it comes to decision-making around the children, it's women, by and large. Ninety percent of primary school educators are women. Most social service fields are also filled with women.

In our culture, women's power is not based entirely on money. Women now have a choice of roles. And to take that a little bit further, men's form of sexist imprisonment has to do with having to work for money and not having a choice about it. Many men feel they have absolutely no choice at all. If you don't have a job and you're not paid well, then you're not fulfilling your role as a man.

Which do you think is more evenly distributed, patriarchal power among men or matriarchal power among women?

It would seem that matriarchal power is more evenly distributed. The male domain is pretty stratified. There are not very many men at the top. There are only a few thousand senators and CEOs. And what's also true about those men at the top is that almost every one of them has a woman partner enabling him to stay up there. Most men who are making lots of money are in partnership with women who are benefiting from that wealth. That's another way women co-create what we call patriarchy.

You mentioned that men are beginning to be concerned about the current scapegoating of men and masculinity. I want to ask you about that, but first I want to ask what problems men have traditionally scapegoated women for.

Well, there are lots of myths. Eve was responsible for the downfall of the human race. Pandora opened the box and let all the ills of mankind come out. Men have been terribly afraid of women's capacity to draw them away from their intent, their goal, and cause their downfall. They fear that women will lead them into "sin." I think it's very deeply ingrained in our culture that there's a lot to be afraid of in women, that there's something about women's erotic and emotional power that's scary.

One of the things that seems most frightening to me about female power is that it is widely denied. You can't trust somebody who's holding a club and saying, "What club? I don't have a club."

Yes, I think that's true. I think that men are taught to be more up-front and overt in their aggression, in their demands for what they want. Women are taught to smile while they're saying no, to smile while they're being contrary, to always put on a pleasant face. If women can't direct their desires, their goals and their will overtly, then they'll do it covertly. Covert power and covert misuse of power are harder to name, harder to identify. We have to look around the edges to see it, because when a person can't direct his or her will straightforwardly, it comes out around the edges as passive aggressiveness. And women are masters at passive-aggressive behavior. Women will needle, women will pick at a man until he goes nuts.

So rather than slugging somebody for one second with a ten-pound weight, they'll . . .

Jab you with a little sharp thing over and over and over again. And it doesn't seem like it's hurting, but after awhile all of a sudden you notice that you're being jabbed with a little sharp thing. And you freak out. But the woman says, "I was just jabbing a little."

And the guy will hear, "Lighten up. Can't you take it?"

And it's tricky because we double-bind each other—men and women alike. I don't want to pathologize women more than men here. We both do this. There are lots of double binds. When women are up-front about what they want, they're considered unfeminine, just as when a man is up-front about what he feels, he's considered a wimp. Every time a woman says, "This is what I want today, this is what I need, this is how I'd like to create this situation," she's going against her socialization and often gets the feedback from the man or from her culture that this is not acceptable, she's being a bitch. We need to acknowledge these double binds and work to see how we can do something different together.

Now, what problems are women scapegoating men for these days?

I think that almost all women—and I don't think I'm overgeneralizing here—when their relationship is not going well, they usually think that it's the man's fault. Often you hear it's his incapacity for intimacy.

What's the attraction of taking that position, rather than taking a good, honest, balanced look at the situation to come up with the best possible solution?

Well, you're blameless. You can be feeling terrible because you're not where you want to be, but it's not your fault. So your self-esteem is still intact.

But if you really had self-esteem, your self-esteem could take a little assault, couldn't it?

That's probably true. If you're not shame-based, you can take a little criticism and work with it, and learn from it.

Are you suggesting, then, that in personal relationships, many women are filled with shame and that's the reason they can't stand self-examination or criticism or accepting of responsibility?

Yes, and it's true for men, too. That's one of the things Aaron and I work with in our workshops around the country: how we can become accountable to each other without going into our shame.

What are women ashamed of?

A classic thing is when a woman and a man are having an argument, the allegation is that she's overwhelming him with her need for attention, her desire for more intimacy. She'll do one of two things. Either she'll think that she's completely wrong or, as a defensive reaction, she'll make him completely wrong.

What would be a better way to approach it?

To be able to acknowledge that we each have a valid perspective, that she's not wrong for wanting more attention, that that's her mandate for being a woman—to want to be in connection all the time. There's nothing wrong with that, but he can't meet her need right now. Does that make him wrong? No. Instead of viewing him as deficient, we can simply say that he's choosing not to do what she wants right now because he wants to do something else. And there's nothing wrong with that, either. So now we have two mutually exclusive wants. A good solution would be to work out a negotiation that says, "Well, I can't give you what you need right now, and I hear your need, and I love you, and let's set a time for later." Neither was wrong; there was just a difference. That's just one small example, but that same kind of negotiation could happen in many, many arenas. That's the difference between creating gender war and gender peace.

This is the idea of partnership?

Yes. It has a lot to do with this paradox of difference—two people, two nations, two cultures, two genders being different—and asking how we negotiate the difference.

What needs to be present before this partnership dynamic can take place? What needs to be present on both sides?

It's what we call gender ground, a positive sense of yourself as a woman or as a man, a sense of value.

So you need a good sense of yourself. But I can imagine a situation in which two people both think they're individually wonderful but they don't . . .

Then you don't have relationship. A partnership assumes some common ground that two people are sharing; each person is intrinsically of equal worth to the other. Different, but of equal worth.

In political rhetoric today, on the macro level of men and women throwing bombs at each other, do you think that women have a healthy respect for men?

Mostly not, not in the rhetoric, not in the media. There's definitely a war going on. But it's interesting for me to notice as I go around the country that there are many, many women who aren't engaged in that war. What we hear most audibly, the most vocal voice in the media, is the feminist movement. A lot of good things have come from the feminist movement, and I want to acknowledge that, but we're not hearing this huge unspoken voice of the many, many women across the country who are in relationship with men, who have male children, who are struggling with career and home and children and relationships, who don't feel represented by the antimale feminist platform. Their voice is unheard.

It is bad for women to always see themselves as victims. The flip side for men seems just as bad—to never see themselves as victims.

Yes. It is ingrained in men to be heroes. In Jungian psychology it's called a split archetype. There are two halves of the same dynamic: victim/victimizer, or you could call it the victim and the hero. Men are desperately burdened with having to be the hero, and women are desperately burdened with having to be the princess.

In order to be the hero, you have to ignore your pain, you have to ignore the fact that you really want to go home, you don't want to work until nine o'clock tonight just to please the boss. You have to ignore your body, your physical discomfort, your emotional discomfort. Men's feelings and needs and desires and dreams exist even though most men are not given permission to pay attention to them, so they come out in addictive and antisocial behaviors.

> There is a certain beauty and romantic sense of great destiny that comes through surrendering to the image—or archetype—of the Hero. For a time we may feel powerful and invulnerable. But there is also a heavy price to pay: alienation, isolation, stress-induced physical or mental illness, injury, and an early death—to name a few consequences.
>
> AARON KIPNIS, Ph.D.
> *Knights Without Armor*

Sometimes when a man expresses his needs, he might be expressing needs that conflict with the woman's needs. If he's not yet in a partnership in which the differences can be negotiated, what can we say to the man to encourage him not to be intimidated by the potential conflict?

What comes off the top of my head is to get together with other men, so that you know you're not alone. If you're all alone and you have a need, and you're with a woman who's saying, "I don't like your need. I think your need is not okay. It doesn't go along with my program," then you may not have enough personality strength to withstand that. You may feel, "God, I must be wrong, because she says something else." But if you have a men's group or you have good men friends who say, "We have that need too," then you've got added strength. It's not just a personal problem. And women need that kind of support as well. I really believe that both sexes need lots of connection with their own gender.

I want to follow up a bit on the idea of men being able to see themselves as victims. The idea of victimhood is a very tricky one, because on the one hand we don't want men to pretend that they've got no problems, but on the other hand we don't want men to wallow in victimhood and say, "Oh, poor us." How can we show men that there is a middle ground between wallowing in victimhood and denying that they have any problems at all?

Just as with women, becoming aware of our victimization is a good and necessary developmental stage you want to visit, but you don't want to take up residence there. We need to stop trying to compete with each other for victim status, and acknowledge the mutual wound we *all* have.

Another fine line that men have to walk is the line between asking women to take responsibility for their part in a problem and blaming women for the whole problem. Do you have any thoughts or guidance about the difference between the two?

That's the essence of the current conversation in the mental health professions around family violence. But if women take responsibility for their contribution to the problem, for many people that equates with "blaming the victim." It's a big question. I think the only answer is that all parties involved have to do the work together. It can't happen in a vacuum. The victim/victimizer, the hero/princess dynamics have to be unwound together.

Do you think one of the things that makes people so reluctant to accept responsibility is because up till now it's been an all-or-nothing game?

That's our expectation. If I want to come out and say, "It's true that I verbally abuse my husband," how can I do that without feeling totally shamed and totally responsible? I can do it because my husband is standing right there face-to-face saying, "Yes, that's true. I receive and acknowledge the truth of that. And I manipulate you with my silence." Together they can say, "This is the game that we play. Let's try not to do it. Let's see if we can do something else and let's have compassion for each other when we do it."

And as soon as you get into the "he started it, she started it" game, you get into that same old actor/reactor, victim/victimizer, all-or-nothing mode.

Yes. So what we need to do in terms of our gender situation is acknowledge that we have a mess here. We have something that's not working. It's not working for a lot of reasons. There are a lot of old patterns that are on their way out, but we don't know what the new ones are, so there's a lot of confusion in our expectations of ourselves as well as the other gender. So let's look at this mess that we're in together and acknowledge that it's painful and it's destructive at times, that we'd like to do better, and we'd like to assist each other in doing better. We don't want to be blamed for it, but, yeah, we probably do contribute to the problem, so let's talk about it. As partners. People who trust each other.

A Final Word

The women who participated in *Good Will Toward Men* have let a genie out of its bottle. They have put at our disposal a powerful tool—a vocabulary, a literature of phrases, ideas, metaphors and fables for perceiving, understanding and discussing gender issues in exciting and promising new ways.

Here are my hopes for what this conceptual shift can accomplish:

- Commonplaces like "It's a man's world" and "Men have all the power" will no longer seem unassailably true.
- Fewer men will mutter "Nothing" when asked "What's wrong, dear?" or spend their time with other men avoiding conversations about what's really on their minds.
- More women will speak up for fairness and magnanimity the way the women in this book have spoken.

Someone once said that men's greatest weakness is their facade of strength, while women's greatest strength is their facade of weakness. My most fervent wish is that this book will help us do away with our fake fronts and get about the business of building a social structure more beautiful and solid than we've ever known.

Resources

BOOKS

Several of the women interviewed for *Good Will Toward Men* have written books.

They are mentioned in the introductory paragraphs in each chapter.

A Circle of Men: The Original Manual for Men's Support Groups, Bill Kauth. New York: St. Martin's Press, 1992.

Fatherhood U.S.A., Debra Klinman, Rhiana Kohl and the Fatherhood Project at the Bank Street College of Education. New York: Garland, 1984 (out of print, but may be available in libraries).

The Hazards of Being Male: Surviving the Myth of Masculine Privilege, Herb Goldberg. New York: NAL-Dutton, 1977.

King, Warrior, Magician, Lover, Robert Moore and Douglas Gillette. San Francisco: Harper, 1991.

Knights Without Armor, Aaron Kipnis. Los Angeles: Jeremy P. Tarcher, 1991.

The Liberated Man, Warren Farrell. New York: Berkley Books, 1993.

Men Freeing Men: Exploding the Myth of the Traditional Male, Francis Baumli, editor. Jersey City: New Atlantis Press, 1985.

The Myth of Male Power: Why Men Are the Disposable Sex, Warren Farrell. New York: Simon and Schuster, 1993.

The Myth of the Monstrous Male and Other Feminist Fables, John Gordon. New York: Playboy Press, 1982 (out of print, but may be available in libraries).

Naked at Gender Gap: A Man's View of the War Between the Sexes, Asa Baber. New York: Birch Lane Press, 1992.

A Nation of Victims, Charles J. Sykes. New York: St. Martin's Press, 1992.

The Nurturing Father, Kyle D. Pruett. New York: Warner Books, 1988 (out of print, but may be available in libraries).

Quiet Desperation: The Truth About Successful Men, Jan Halper. New York: Warner Books, 1989.

What Men Really Want, Herb Goldberg. New York: Signet, 1991.

Why Men Are the Way They Are, Warren Farrell. New York: Berkley Books, 1988.

Wingspan: Inside the Men's Movement, Chris Harding, editor. New York: St. Martin's Press, 1992.

PERIODICALS

Publications issued by organizations listed under the Organizations heading, below, are not shown under this heading.

This is, of necessity, an abbreviated list.
Menstuff: The National Men's Resource Calendar, below, offers a wide-ranging list of over ninety publications.

When writing for information, kindly include a self-addressed, stamped envelope.

Full-Time Dads: The Journal for Caregiving Fathers
P.O. Box 577
Cumberland Center, ME 04021
humor, fiction, personal experiences

Journeymen
513 Chester Turnpike
Candia, NH 03034
everything about men

The Liberator
17854 Lyons Street
Forest Lake, MN 55025-8854
militant, legal focus

Men As We Are
581 Tenth Street
Brooklyn, NY 11215-4401
men's literature, news and commentary

Menstuff: The National Men's Resource Calendar
P.O. Box 800-GW
San Anselmo, CA 94979
information, events, resources and reviews

Reflections for Women
11215 46 Avenue
Edmonton, Alberta T6H 0A2
CANADA
extra postage required for international mail; include international
postage coupon or Canadian stamps with self-addressed envelope
for reply

Wingspan: Journal of the Male Spirit
P.O. Box 23550
Brightmoor Station
Detroit, MI 48223
mythopoetic; extensive event calendar

ORGANIZATIONS

All of these organizations welcome
the participation and support of both sexes.

When writing for information, kindly include
a self-addressed, stamped envelope.
Most of these organizations are underfunded and understaffed.

American Men's Studies Association
22 East Street
Northampton, MA 01060
Scholarly, Multidisciplinary forum on men's issues

Children's Rights Council
220 I Street NE, Room 230
Washington, DC 20002-4307
(202) 547-6227
advocating children's right to two parents

Committee on Gender Bias in the Courts
P.O. Box 50
Punta Gorda, FL 33951
(813) 637-7477
works to require judicial gender bias task forces to address bias
against both sexes

Concerned Black Men
655 Fifteenth Street NW, Suite 300
Washington, DC 20005
(202) 639-4052
African-American male social issues

Feminists for Men
P.O. Box 17944
Boulder, CO 80908
(303) 938-8632
promale feminism

Joint Custody Association
10606 Wilkins Avenue
Los Angeles, CA 90024
(310) 475-5352
legislative efforts for joint custody

Men's Education Network International
Box 10033
Kansas City, MO 64111
(816) 561-4066
general men's issues internationally

Men's Health Network
P.O. Box 770
Washington, DC 20044
(202) 543-MHN1
men's physical and emotional health issues

Men's Rights, Inc.
P.O. Box 163180
Sacramento, CA 95816
(916) 484-7333
general men's issues

Movement for the Establishment of Real Gender Equality
10011 116 Street, Suite 501
Edmonton, Alberta T5K 1V4
CANADA
(403) 488-4593
gender issues in Canada
extra postage required for international mail; include international
postage coupon or Canadian stamps with self-addressed envelope
for reply

National Black Men's Health Network
250 Georgia Avenue, Suite 321
Atlanta, GA 30312
(404) 524-7237
African-American male health issues

National Center for Men
P.O. Box 317
Brooklyn NY 11240
(718) 845-2010
general men's issues

National Coalition of Free Men
P.O. Box 129
Manhasset, NY 11030
(516) 482-6378
general men's issues

National Congress for Men and Children
2020 Pennsylvania Avenue NW, Suite 277
Washington, DC 20006-1846
(202) FATHERS
"preserving the promise of fatherhood" after divorce

National Council of African-American Men
c/o Center for Black Leadership Development and Research
University of Kansas
Lawrence, KS 66045
(913) 864-3990
umbrella organization for black male concerns

National Organization for Men
11 Park Place
New York, NY 10007
(212) 686-MALE
general men's issues

Northwest Feminist Anti-Censorship Taskforce
15911 Westminster Way N., #300
Seattle, WA 98133
(206) 292-1159
feminist opposition to censorship of erotica

100 Black Men of America, Inc.
127 Peachtree Street, Suite 704
Atlanta, GA 30303
(404) 525-7111
African-American male social issues

Women's Freedom Network
Box 179
4410 Massachusetts Avenue, NW
Washington, DC 20016
(202) 885-2965
political issues

Women's International Network for Healthy Relationships
250 Bishop's Way, Suite 301
Brookfield, WI 53005
(414) 821-1709
relationship issues

INSTITUTES, SERVICES AND PRACTICES
MENTIONED IN GOOD WILL TOWARD MEN

Carolyn Baker, Ph.D.
1901 Cleveland Avenue #2
Santa Rosa, CA 95401
(707) 545-8151

Audrey B. Chapman
A. B. Chapman Associates, Inc.
P.O. Box 383
Washington, DC 20059
(703) 914-2068

Elizabeth Herron and Aaron Kipnis, Ph.D.
Santa Barbara Institute for Gender Studies
P.O. Box 4782
Santa Barbara, CA 93140
(805) 963-8285

Laurie Ingraham, MSW
Addictive Relationships Center
250 Bishop's Way, Suite 301
Brookfield, WI 53005
(414) 821-1709

New Warrior Network
8426 N. Regent Rd.
Fox Point, WI 53217
(414) 228-6810

Judith Sherven, Ph.D. and James Sniechowski
The Menswork Center
1950 Sawtelle Boulevard, Suite 340
Los Angeles, CA 90025
(310) 479-2749

Char Tosi
Woman Within
P.O. Box 131
Oak Creek, WI 53154
(414) 762-7727

Computer Networking

CompuServe
go issues, select men's issues section; GO HSX100

Delphi
type: groups, select mensnet

Internet
to join mail-men, send message to: mail-men-requests @ usl.com

Prodigy
jump: health, select health and life-styles, select bulletin board, select men's issues

Video

Heroes & Strangers
Lorna Rasmussen and Tony Heriza
New Day Films
121 West Twenty-seventh Street, Suite 902
New York, NY 10001
(212) 645-8210
rental or purchase
a sympathetic look at fathers

About the Author

JACK KAMMER launched a radio talk show called *In a Man's Shoes* in 1983. Since then he has been one of America's most colorful and incisive commentators on issues between men and women. He has testified on gender issues before committees in both houses of Congress, appeared on innumerable radio and TV shows—even tried stand-up comedy to present a new perspective on trouble between the sexes—and has written for such publications as *USA Today*, the *New York Daily News* and *Playboy*. He was born, raised and now lives in Baltimore.